I0211923

Getting Started as a Freelance Interpreter

Essential strategies for launching and growing your
business as a spoken-language interpreter

Corinne McKay

Copyright © 2025 Corinne McKay

All rights reserved. No part of this publication may be reproduced, distributed, or transmitted in any form or by any means, including photocopying, recording, or other electronic or mechanical methods, without the prior written permission of the publisher, except in the case of brief quotations embodied in critical reviews and certain other noncommercial uses permitted by copyright law.

ISBN: 979-8-9917616-6-6 (Paperback)

ISBN: 979-8-9917616-7-3 (Hardcover)

ISBN: 979-8-9917616-8-0 (EPUB)

TILT
PUBLISHING

Tilt Publishing
700 Park Offices Drive, Suite 250
Research Triangle, NC 27709

Getting Started as a
Freelance
Interpreter

*Essential Strategies for Launching and Growing
Your Business as a Spoken-language Interpreter*

Corinne McKay

Table of Contents

Introduction

Interpreting is an exciting and dynamic career, offering the chance to bridge language gaps in real-time, help people communicate across cultures, and work in diverse settings—from courtrooms to hospitals to international conferences. But getting started can feel overwhelming. What training do you need? How do you find clients? What can you expect from your first interpreting assignments?

This book is here to help. It's not a deep dive into every aspect of interpreting—that would take volumes—but rather a practical guide to getting started. Whether you're brand new to the field or transitioning from another language-related profession, this book will walk you through the key steps to launching a freelance interpreting career.

I write this as someone who has been where you are. I started my freelance career in 2002 as a French to English (written) translator, earning my American Translators Association certification in 2003. While I did some community and court interpreting early on—and loved it—life circumstances and the lack of remote interpreting options at the time made it difficult to pursue. For over 15 years, I worked exclusively as a translator, but I never lost the desire to return to interpreting. Eventually, I did.

Now, with five years of interpreting experience and two decades in the language professions, I want to share what I've learned to help you navigate the first steps of this journey. If you're interested in spoken-language interpreting, this book will give you the foundation you need. And if written translation is more your focus, you might enjoy my other book, *How to Succeed as a Freelance Translator*, available at trainingfortranslators.com.

As I mentioned above, I was always interpreting-curious, but for more than 15 years, I took no action on my big interpreting dream. At the 2018 American Translators Association conference, I attended a presentation on consecutive interpreting by Athena Matilsky (athenaskyinterpreting.com), an English/Spanish/French interpreter and interpreter trainer. The session was great, and afterward, I had a bit of a "now or never" moment. At age 47, I thought, "I don't have to do this, but if I ever want to do it, I need to start taking action now." After that conference, I started working with Athena one-on-one, with the goal of passing the State of Colorado's French court interpreter exam. I was really starting from ground zero: I had a lot of work to do on my spoken French before I could even start learning proper interpreting technique. If you're a beginning interpreter and need some perspective, here it is: one of the most basic techniques that beginning interpreters learn as a precursor to simultaneous interpreting is called shadowing. Shadowing (sometimes referred to as "parroting") means that you listen to a piece of audio (the radio news, a speech, a podcast, etc.) and repeat after the speaker in the same language; it's like simultaneous interpreting without the language transfer, and it's how you learn to listen and talk at the same time. When I started my interpreter training, my spoken French was so rusty and slow that I could barely even shadow: I typically had to either slow YouTube videos down to 75% speed, or use materials for French learners with slow, clear speakers.

To make a long story short (more details appear through-out the book), I passed the Colorado court interpreter exam in 2019, started working as a contract interpreter for the Colorado Judicial Branch, and had the idea that "someday" I'd like to pur-sue a Master's in conference interpreting. At that time, the main roadblocks were the lack of conference interpreting programs and conference interpreting work near where I live. I definitely didn't anticipate that a global pandemic would resolve both of those roadblocks: all of a sudden, there were multiple online con-ference interpreting degree programs to choose from, and many more options for remote interpreting work. In August of 2020, I passed the advanced entry exams for the Glendon College/York University Master of Conference Interpreting program, which meant that I could do the degree in one year. After a very gruel-ing 10 months of working part-time and attending the Glendon program full-time, I passed the exit exams in July of 2021, and immediately started looking for conference interpreting work. At this writing, three years later, I'm very satisfied with the quality and quantity of conference interpreting work that I've found and I'm enjoying it a great deal. I'm very happy with the interpreting path that I've pursued over the past five years, and I hope that what I've learned will be useful to you as you read this book.

Differences Between This Book and *How to Succeed as a Freelance Translator*

I am also the author of *How to Succeed as a Freelance Translator*. That book is intended as a much more comprehensive guide to the marketing, legal, and management aspects of running a freelance business, while this book is intended for:

- Beginning and aspiring interpreters. Experienced interpreters may find some useful information here, but the book is aimed primarily at early-career interpreters.

- Interpreters seeking information about the interpreting profession, rather than about freelancing in general. If you're interested in big-picture information about running a freelance business as a translator or interpreter, visit my website trainingfortranslators.com, where there are over 1,050 blog posts you can read for free!

Additionally, this book is much more U.S.-specific than *How to Succeed as a Freelance Translator*. Information about interpreter certification is specific to the U.S. I present some general information about the European market, but most of what I've written about here is based on my work as a U.S.-based interpreter.

CHAPTER 1

The Essentials of Freelance Interpreting

1.1 What Is Interpreting?

Later in this book, you'll learn in more detail about the various modes of interpreting. For now, here's what you need to know: **Translators write, interpreters talk.** The subject of this book is interpreting, or spoken-language work. It's a confusing distinction; even reputable news outlets repeatedly use the expression "speaking through a translator" (you can't…translators sit in front of the computer and don't talk to anyone!) Additionally, many languages—but not English—simply use the term "spoken translation," which is less confusing. But for our purposes in this book, just remember that we're talking exclusively about spoken language work.

1.2 Language Skills

An interpreter's most crucial skill is, obviously, understanding and speaking at least two languages. There are other skills on the must-have list, but you really can't work as an interpreter without language skills.

Many beginning interpreters wonder, "Just how good do my language skills have to be?" The answer is, of course, "really, really good." But the specifics depend on what languages you speak and what markets you're planning on working in. For example, in the U.S., it is generally expected that most interpreters are bidirectional/biactive, meaning they interpret in both directions (i.e. English to Spanish and Spanish to English). In settings such as courts and hospitals, it is critical for the interpreter to be bidirectional, because they are always interpreting back and forth between various parties. In conference settings, it is more common for the assignment to be *primarily* in one direction (interpreting English into French for a conference that happens in the U.S. with participants from Canada, for example) with some bidirectionality (for example, if the non-English-speaking delegates want to ask questions). But in the U.S., it is relatively uncommon for interpreters to have a "passive" language, meaning a language they interpret only from, not into. And many, if not most interpreters in the U.S., have only one language combination; at the very least, it is not considered at all odd in the U.S. market to have only one language combination.

The situation in Europe is different: medical and court interpreting are less formalized in many European countries, or may be lumped into a broader category called "public service interpreting." It is more common for interpreters in Europe to interpret into their native language only, as translators in the U.S. typically do. It's also more common for interpreters in Europe to interpret from multiple passive languages into only one active language, for example from French, Spanish, Italian, and Portuguese into English.

There are also interpreters (known as "double A" in the conference interpreting world) who are native speakers of more than one language: people who grew up speaking one language at home and another at school, or who spoke two languages at home, or who moved between countries during childhood. It's definitely possible to work as an interpreter without having language skills at that level, but it's also true that if you want to work on the U.S. market (where bidirectional interpreting is the norm) and you're a native English speaker who learned your non-native language primarily in school, you may need to do some significant work on your language skills before you can consider interpreting professionally.

1.3 A, B, and C Languages

In the translation world, languages are referred to as source (the "from" language) and target (the "into" language). Many translators (who work with the written word) work in only one language combination (for example French to English, or English to Japanese). In the interpreting world, the situation is different, typically using the following language designations:

- A: the interpreter's native language/mother tongue; interpreters who truly are native speakers of more than one language are often referred to as "double A," or having two A languages.

- B: a non-native language that the interpreter works both from and into; for example, a native English speaker who is a non-native speaker of German, and interprets both from and into German, would be referred to as an English A/ German B interpreter.

- C: a non-native language that the interpreter works from, but not into; more commonly seen on the European market, an interpreter might have one C language (for example,

French A, English B, Spanish C) or may work from multiple C languages into an A language with no B language (for example, French A, Spanish C, English C, Russian C).

Another convention that differs from the translation world to the interpreting world is the idea of working into your native language only. In the U.S. translation market, the vast majority of translators work into their native language only. It's really only in cases where a native speaker of the target language is very hard to find (for example, a translation from Thai into English) that a non-native speaker might be used. In the interpreting world, particularly in the U.S., this convention is much less applicable. Most interpreters work in both directions, and some interpreters may even prefer working into their non-native or B language because they are virtually guaranteed to understand everything the speaker says, which is often less true when interpreting from a non-native language.

1.4 Interpreter Certification in the U.S.

In the U.S., there are more specialized certifications available for interpreters than for translators. For some interpreters, such as Spanish court interpreters, certification may be mandatory at the state or federal levels. For conference interpreters, there really is no standard certification (but see below for other options), and for some interpreters, certification may be a plus but not a must. Following is a brief overview of the certification options available for interpreters in the U.S.

State Court Interpreter Certification

- If you would like to become a state-certified court interpreter, the best place to start is your state judicial branch's office of language access or the closest equivalent department. There, you should be able to find out your state's process for becoming certified, and whether certification is available in your language pair(s). Many, but not all, states use the interpreter certification exams developed by the National Center for State Courts (ncsc. org), through its CLAC (Consortium of Language Access Coordinators), formerly known as the Consortium. Other states (most notably, New York and California) use their own tests. Many states require that you first complete an orientation, then a written exam, then an oral exam. However, the specifics vary from state to state: some states put a limit on how often, or how many times, you can take each component of the exam, or how many times you can re-take the exam if you fail, or whether you can re-take only the components that you failed, versus re-taking the whole exam. The NCSC has oral exams for 17 languages, which you can view in the Interpreter Resources section of their website. The NCSC also produces a practice examination (only available in Spanish or language-neutral/all-English) that is an excellent resource if you're preparing for a state-level court interpreter certification exam. Most state-level exams (including the NCSC exams) will include sight translation in both directions, consecutive in both directions (for example, a conversation between a witness and an attorney, where the actor playing the attorney speaks English and the actor playing the witness speaks your other language), and simultaneous into your non-English language only.

Federal Court Interpreter Certification

- In the U.S., the federal Court Interpreter Certification Examination (FCICE) is offered for Spanish/English only and is a fairly long process. For current information, visit their website (uscourts.gov/services-forms/ federal-court-interpreters/federal-court-interpreter- certification-examination). The first step is a multiple-choice test in English and Spanish taken on a computer, with your scores returned the same day. The second and more challenging step is the oral examination, including sight translation, consecutive interpreting, and simultaneous interpreting. The testing process is currently administered by a contractor called Prometric, and you can find more information on their website (prometric.com/test- takers/search/aousc) which also includes a practice exam and an examinee handbook. Becoming federally certified is an excellent goal for Spanish interpreters, as it has become somewhat of a gold standard for Spanish court and legal interpreting and can open the door to a lot of work. It's important to prepare yourself for a fairly lengthy process since the written and oral exams are often administered in alternating years. You may also want to take a prep course or join a practice group. The University of Arizona's Court Interpreter Training Institute (nci.arizona.edu/interpreter- training/court-interpreter-training-institute-citi) and the National Association of Judiciary Interpreters and Translators (najit.org) are good places to start.

Healthcare Interpreter Certification

- Through the Certification Commission for Healthcare Interpreters (cchicertification.org). CCHI offers three healthcare interpreter credentials: the non-language-specific

CoreCHI ™ credential, the non-language-specific CoreCHI Performance™ credential (involving an English-to-English interpreting performance exam), and the CHI™ credential, available to Spanish, Arabic, and Mandarin interpreters. The bilingual CHI exam includes four consecutive interpreting passages, two simultaneous passages, three sight translation passages, and a multiple-choice translation section.

As of 2024, the CoreCHI™ test can be taken at any time, either in-person at a testing center or online, and the initial application/testing fee is $231. The English-to-English and bilingual CHI™ tests must be taken at a Prometric testing center, within a specific time window specified by CCHI (see their website for dates), and requires the $231 payment for the initial application fee plus a fee of $302 for the CHI exam.

- If you're looking for something more in-depth than a webinar but less committing than a certification or degree program, you might want to take a look at interpreter training programs such as Bridging the Gap (offered by various entities, developed by the Cross-Cultural Health Care Program (xculture.org/bridging-the-gap) or The Community Interpreter (thecommunityinterpreter.com/). Bridging the Gap is a 40 or 64-hour medical interpreter training program; the longer program includes modules on interpreting in mental health settings and for LGBTQIA communities. Courses offered through the Cross-Cultural Health Care Program cost $795 and run for 10 consecutive days, four hours per day. Other entities offer other types of schedules: the Academy of Interpretation (academyofinterpretation.com/product/bridging-the-gap) offers sessions that meet eight hours a day for five days;

current tuition is $685. The Community Interpreter is a 40-hour course in community interpreting currently being offered online, with most sessions running eight hours a day for five days.

- The U.S. Department of State has many opportunities for freelance interpreters (state.gov/freelance-linguists-ols/). The interpreting division in the Office of Language Services handles the screening and testing of interpreters at three levels: liaison, seminar, and conference (see the link above for descriptions of what these mean). The Department of State uses contract interpreters for travel assignments and for on-site assignments in Washington. Unlike the process to be tested as a court interpreter, the Department of State process has no set dates or deadlines; you simply apply via their website and wait for them to contact you if they need your language combination. The link above has sample speeches you can use to assess the interpreting skill level required for each level of interpreting.

- Lastly, there are two professional associations for conference interpreters that function almost like certifications, because they require peer recommendations in order to become a full member. AIIC (aiic.org/), the International Association of Conference Interpreters/ *Association Internationale des Interprètes de Conférence* is headquartered in Geneva, Switzerland, and is open to conference interpreters with at least 150 days in the booth, plus sponsorship from current AIIC interpreters who have been Active members for at least five years. Whether membership in AIIC is achievable or beneficial really depends on where you work and who you work with. Start by reading the information at aiic.org/site/ interpreter/active-members and consider becoming an

AIIC Pre-Candidate if you don't yet meet the requirements but may in the future. TAALS (taals.net/), the American Association of Language Specialists, accepts both translators and interpreters as members, and uses a similar sponsorship system to AIIC, but only 100 days of conference interpreting experience are required.

1.5 Professional Associations for Interpreters

Belonging to a professional association for interpreters can be a big boost to your interpreting career in terms of the contacts you can make within the association, the credibility of being a member of a professional association, and the professional development opportunities that many associations offer.

Because you have to pay dues to belong to a professional association, membership shows a commitment to professionalism. Even if you are not or cannot be certified by a professional association, belonging to one shows that you are serious about your interpreting career. You may want to take a look at some of the following associations:

- The American Translators Association/ATA (atanet.org) welcomes interpreters as members and has an Interpreters' Division. Membership in ATA is open to anyone "with an interest in translation and interpreting as a profession or as a scholarly pursuit." You do not have to apply or be sponsored for membership, and membership is open to residents of any country, not just the U.S. As of this writing (2024), ATA's individual membership dues are $249 per year, and there are various other member categories for students, businesses, and institutions. ATA certifies translators, not interpreters, but does offer the Credentialed Interpreter (CI) designation that can be displayed on your ATA directory profile if you have passed another entity's interpreter certification exam, or if you are a member of a sponsorship-based association for interpreters, such as AIIC or TAALS (see above for more information on these associations). ATA also has many local and regional chapters that welcome interpreters and are relatively inexpensive to join. ATA has a multitude of professional development opportunities including a webinar series and an annual conference.

- The National Association of Judiciary Interpreters and Translators/NAJIT (najit.org) is an organization primarily for court interpreters, but "anyone with an interest in the field of legal interpreting and translating or who shares NAJIT's interests and objectives is welcome to join." Individual membership in NAJIT as of this writing is $125, and there are various other membership categories for organizations, students, or two members at the same address. NAJIT has a webinar series and an annual conference.

- For information on AIIC and TAALS, see the previous section on interpreter certification.

- The American Association of Interpreters and Translators in Education/AAITE (aaite.org/) is a relatively new but active association exclusively for educational interpreters and translators. As of this writing, AAITE's individual membership is $60 a year, and they are holding a webinar series of "Edu-Talks" and a national conference.

1.6 Modes of Interpreting: Consecutive Interpreting, Simultaneous Interpreting, Sight Translation, and a Few Other Terms

Before beginning your interpreting journey, you should be familiar with the various modes of interpreting and how they are used in real-life situations.

- In **consecutive interpreting**, only one person talks at a time. Actually, in reality, people talk over each other all the time in consecutive interpreting situations, but the idea of consec is that the speaker talks, then pauses while the interpreter talks, interpreting what the speaker said. This could range from just a few words, for example, a doctor asking a patient, "What is your date of birth?" Or, in a diplomatic interpreting situation, a speaker might give an entire speech while the interpreter takes notes and then interprets. These are sometimes referred to as **short dialogue interpreting** (typically seen in court, medical, educational, and community settings) and **long consecutive interpreting** (typically seen in diplomatic and conference settings, with speeches ranging from 5-20 minutes). Consecutive interpreting often requires note-taking. For short dialogue interpreting, note-taking may be less critical, but it's an extremely useful skill to learn, particularly for settings like court and medical where there's a lot of detailed information. For long consecutive interpreting, note-taking is essential, and is a key skill that conference interpreters put a great deal of time into learning and practicing. An advantage of consecutive interpreting is that it doesn't require any special equipment if the setting is a small group where everyone can hear each other, and the interpreter does not have to be able to talk and listen at the same time. A disadvantage is that good consecutive interpreting is harder than it looks; it's easy to lose or confuse pieces of information, and people can easily become frustrated with the slow pace of consec and how long it takes to interpret everything. Consecutive interpreting can be a critical skill, or one that you barely ever use. Most community, medical, educational, and court interpreters will do consec at least some of the time, and perhaps all the time. On the other hand, it's not unusual to meet conference interpreters who almost never do consec, and at least some international organizations have moved almost exclusively to simultaneous, even for dialogue-heavy meetings, because consecutive interpreting slows things down and makes the meeting twice as long. Whether you need solid consec really depends on who you work for and how they organize their meetings.

- In **simultaneous interpreting**, the speaker and the interpreter talk at the same time. The interpreter maintains a certain amount of lag, or décalage, so that they can formulate a complete idea before speaking it, but the speaker does not pause to allow the interpreter to interpret. If you've seen the interpreters with headsets on at the United Nations or in similar settings, that's simul! Simultaneous interpreting is easy to describe and very time-consuming to learn. The first step in learning simul is a skill called **shadowing**, where you repeat after a speaker, in the same language (like "simultaneous" without the interpreting). This helps you learn to listen and talk at the same time. An advantage of simultaneous is that it's fast and reduces meeting participants' frustration at having to wait for the interpreter. A disadvantage is that, unless done in a mode called **chuchotage** (French for "whispering") where the interpreter sits in close proximity to their client(s) and speaks in a low tone of voice, simultaneous requires special equipment so the interpreter can hear the speaker and the client(s) can hear the interpreter. This may be portable equipment, sometimes known as **bidule**, or may be a full meeting setup with booths for the interpreters and wireless headsets for the participants, or a remote simultaneous interpreting system, most commonly Zoom or Webex, but sometimes using specialized software designed just for interpreting.

- In **sight translation** (a confusing term, since it doesn't contain the word "interpreting"), the interpreter verbally interprets from a written document. For example, a public defender might give the interpreter a plea agreement and say, "Read this to the defendant in Spanish." Sight translation requires you to interpret while reading ahead, anticipating sentence structure, and scanning for tricky vocabulary. Sight translation is different from **simultaneous interpreting with text**, which is where an interpreter has a written document, typically a speech, but the speaker may not be following the written version word for word. In sim with text, the interpreter has to listen while reading, analyze the written document for differences from the spoken version, and interpret. Most court interpreting exams in the U.S. include sight translation, sometimes only from English into the interpreter's other language.

- The hybrid **sim-consec** mode exists, but doesn't seem to have gained much traction in the market. Sim-consec involves the interpreter recording a speech on a mobile device (phone, tablet, smart watch) while also taking notes, then listening to the recorded speech through a headset or earbuds while referring to their notes and interpreting simultaneously. This method has a lot to recommend it, particularly because a lot of interpreters dislike long consecutive or never learned how to do it well, but it also has various issues: the interpreter has to be close enough to the speaker to get a good recording, participants have to consent to being recorded, and if the recording were to fail and the interpreter has minimal notes, the situation could be a disaster.

1.7 Flavors of Interpreting: Community, Educational, Court, Medical, Conference

You don't have to know right away what type of interpreting you want to do (I did not!), but it helps to have an idea of the various flavors of interpreting and which might appeal or not appeal to you. Each type of interpreting has its pluses and minuses: community interpreting is very much in demand and gives you direct contact with clients who really need your services, but tends not to pay very well; conference interpreting tends to pay quite well, but requires extensive training and either a robust remote interpreting setup, a willingness to travel, or both. Medical and court interpreting may offer interpreters, particularly Spanish interpreters, the possibility of an in-house job, something that's hard to come by in other languages and specializations. It really all depends on your location, languages, income needs, and what type of interpreting you enjoy and are good at.

- **Community interpreters** definitely do consecutive interpreting, probably do sight translation, and may do simultaneous interpreting in certain settings. Community interpreting is a very broad term, encompassing aspects of social services, medical, legal, and educational interpreting.

Some people who serve as community interpreters might not even self-identify as interpreters. Rather, they think of themselves as "the person who speaks English and Navajo," or "the person who helps out when someone speaks only Spanish." It can also be difficult to differentiate between community interpreting and specialized educational, medical, and legal interpreting. An interpreter who helps a parent enroll their child in school might be considered a community interpreter, while an interpreter with a higher level of training who interprets for educational assessments or IEP meetings would be considered an educational interpreter. An interpreter who helps out at a legal aid agency might be considered more of a community interpreter than a court interpreter. If you're particularly interested in community interpreting, The Community Interpreter (thecommunityinterpreter.com) offers various resources and online courses. There is currently no certification specific to community interpreting.

- **Educational interpreters** have recently begun to differentiate themselves as a specialization separate from community interpreting. Educational interpreters generally work in K-12 settings, interpreting for anything from parent-teacher conferences to school board meetings. Educational interpreters will typically be called on to do consecutive interpreting and sight translation, and may provide simultaneous interpreting for larger-scale meetings. There is currently no certification specific to educational interpreting.

- **Court interpreters** work in all types of court settings, from city, county, and state courts to federal courts, and in private-sector settings such as depositions and attorney-client conferences. Court interpreters do consecutive and simultaneous interpreting and sight translation, with the bulk of their work in the courtroom consisting of simultaneous interpreting into their non-English language for defendants with limited English proficiency. Court interpreting often requires certification at the state or federal level if it is available for your language, and some sort of registration or approval process if certification is not available. In many parts of the U.S., it is now difficult to impossible to find work as a Spanish court interpreter if you are not certified. Prior to COVID, court interpreting was done almost exclusively in person, then went almost exclusively remote for the next two years, and is now (like many things!) in a hybrid situation. To get the maximum amount of work as a court interpreter, you need to be able to work both remotely and in person. If you're interested in pursuing certification as a court interpreter, start with your state Judicial Branch's office of language access, or the closest similar department.

- **Medical interpreters** work in a variety of medical settings such as doctors' offices and hospitals. Medical interpreters do consecutive interpreting, sight translation, and may do simultaneous interpreting for meetings or conferences. Medical interpreting requires specialized training (for both the technical and human aspects of the job) and requires the interpreter to remain professional in potentially very emotional situations. Medical interpreters may or may not need to be certified, by either the Certification Commission for Healthcare Interpreters (which offers the Certified Healthcare Interpreter, or CHI™, credential), or the National Board of Certification for Medical Interpreters (which offers the Certified Medical Interpreter, or CMI, credential).

Aspiring medical interpreters might also want to look at the Bridging the Gap 40-hour training program (xculture.org).

- **Conference interpreters** tend to work mostly in settings that require simultaneous interpreting, from business meetings, to diplomatic settings, to professional conferences. Conference interpreting does sometimes involve consecutive and long consecutive interpreting, if the interpreter is called on to interpret an entire speech. But the vast majority of conference interpreting is simultaneous, which requires specialized training and a lot of practice. Government entities such as the U.S. State Department use conference interpreters, as do international institutions such as the United Nations, but conference interpreting might also take the form of a bank's employee town hall, or an NGO's stakeholder meeting, or a community health organization's annual conference. Many conference interpreters hold a Master of Conference Interpreting. If you are interested in pursuing conference interpreting training, a good place to start is the International Association of Conference Interpreters (known by its French acronym, AIIC, at aiic.org).

1.8 Freelancing and Salaried Jobs

One factor to consider before you embark on an interpreting career, particularly in the U.S., is whether you are interested in being a freelancer or if you would prefer a salaried job. This is a key decision because the vast majority of interpreters in the U.S. are freelancers. If you interpret between Spanish and English, there may be full-time positions in medical or court interpreting, and if you live in a major city (particularly New York or Washington, DC) and are a trained professional conference interpreter, you may see salaried positions advertised within government institutions, national security entities, large NGOs, international financial institutions, etc. However, outside those specific situations, it's likely that you will find yourself as a free-lancer working with multiple clients.

Freelancing has its advantages: specifically, the freedom of working when, where, and how you want to, and the ability to set your own rates. However, many freelancers struggle more with the business aspects of their work than with the language aspects. Finding and retaining clients, figuring out how much you need to charge in order to achieve the same level of financial security as someone with a traditional job, balancing remote and in-person interpreting so you have enough work, setting your rates so that you are earning a viable living while having a healthy work vol-ume---all of these things are very challenging if you've never run a business before, which most freelance interpreters have not.

If you are *only* interested in salaried jobs, you should do a sig-nificant amount of research and groundwork before you make the leap to interpreting. Many salaried jobs that pay well are not open to beginners, and many entry-level jobs that require inter-preting skills are going to be more on the level of a call center rep or a bilingual customer service rep. For conference interpret-ers, finding a salaried job may mean being open to moving, even internationally, to a location where salaried jobs are more plen-tiful, such as the hubs of the European Union and international institution epicenters in Brussels and Geneva. Definitely do not embark on an interpreting career with the assumption that there will be a salaried job waiting for you.

1.9 What You Need to Get Started

The space and equipment you need to get started as an interpreter depends a lot on whether you're going to work remotely, in-person, or both. If you're going to work primarily or exclusively in person, you honestly don't need much, unless you work for clients who expect you to provide your own listening and transmitting equipment for on-site interpreting (in most cases, the client will provide this). For in-person work, you may simply need some professional clothing, a notebook (most interpreters use top-bound steno pads), and pens.

For remote interpreting, you'll need a physical space that's conducive to the job, and you'll need a robust technology setup. See this book's section on remote interpreting for more information. At a minimum, you'll need a quiet space, a fast internet connection (I **strongly** recommend using wired internet rather than wi-fi), a computer that can run remote interpreting software, a second monitor, and at least one good headset or a standalone microphone and headphones.

To market your interpreting services, you'll need some sort of web presence: this could be your own website, a LinkedIn profile, and/or a profile in the directory of one or more associations for interpreters. See this book's sections on marketing your interpreting services for more information.

1.10 Tax and Legal Issues

For thorough information about setting up a freelance business in your state and paying taxes as a freelancer, talk to an accountant or attorney who knows your state's requirements well.

Following is a brief look at the tax and legal implications of working as a freelancer in the United States.

Whether you are a contractor (freelancer) or an employee is defined by how you are paid. If you are an employee, you receive an IRS form called a W-2 at the end of the year and your employer pays certain taxes on your behalf. If you are a freelancer, you receive an IRS form called a 1099 and are responsible for paying all your own taxes, and specifically for paying both the employer and the employee portions of certain taxes. Most importantly, you need to:

- Clarify with every client whether you are working for them as an employee or as a contractor
- Save an appropriate amount of your freelance income to pay your taxes and other business expenses
- Establish a set of business bank accounts that are completely separate from your personal bank accounts

It's always painful to hear about freelancers who are either unaware that self-employment tax is a thing, or who earn more than they expected (a good problem to have!) and don't have the funds they need to pay their self-employment tax. This should never happen, if you:

- Deposit your freelance earnings into an account that is separate from your personal funds
- Earmark a percentage of each payment for taxes

Setting up such an account is easy; many banks now allow you to open a new account online, and you don't need a business-specific account unless it gives you some financial advantages. At the very least, just set up a checking and savings account in your own name and use them as your business accounts. Deposit all of your freelance earnings into those accounts. How much to earmark for taxes and business expenses depends on your tax bracket and how much you earn. Unless you are in a very low tax bracket, you should probably reserve at least 30% of your income for taxes. Something more like 40% will definitely cover your taxes and allow you to put some money into retirement and a paid vacation account.

In most U.S. states, you do not have to have a business license or any other formal paperwork in order to do business as a sole proprietor, which is the default business structure for freelancers who haven't explicitly formed a corporation or other entity. The upside is that working as a sole proprietor is easy: you just start earning money as a freelancer (as long as your state doesn't require any other formalities, which most do not). The downside is that, as a sole proprietor, you pay self-employment tax on every cent you earn, and U.S. self-employment tax is a pretty big hit: currently over 15% on top of the taxes you would pay if you worked for an employer—because you pay both the employer and the employee portions of certain taxes.

Incorporating, typically as an S-Corp or LLC (Limited Liability Corporation), can allow you to legally avoid paying self-employment tax on a portion of your income, by assigning some of your income to yourself as "wages" (on which you do pay self-employment tax) and some to the corporation as "profit" (on which you do not pay self-employment tax). Although this distinction is somewhat arbitrary when the corporation consists only of you, it's legal, as long as you pay yourself what the IRS defines as "a reasonable wage." Talk to a good accountant before you set up a corporate structure, but if you make more than about $50,000 per year in self-employment income, this could be a good option for you.

1.11 Your First Year as a Freelancer

Unless you have a built-in client such as a court system that is required to use you, your first year as a freelance interpreter is likely to involve a lot of marketing; perhaps more marketing than interpreting.

Marketing yourself as a freelancer is partially a question of supply and demand: there is a ton of work for Spanish interpreters in the U.S., but there are also a lot of qualified Spanish interpreters. There is a lot less work for Amharic or Tagalog, but there are also far fewer interpreters. Remote interpreting has been a game-changer for interpreters; arguably, the changes have been both positive and negative, but it's true that as a beginning interpreter, your location is no longer as much of a factor as it was pre-2020. It's now possible to find remote interpreting work from almost anywhere with a good internet connection, and you no longer have to move to a major city or live in hotels 300 days a year to find work as a conference interpreter.

I've started from zero as a freelancer-- twice. In 2002/2003, I launched my freelance French to English translation business with a Master's degree in French Literature and not much else; I had very little translation experience, and no contacts in the industry. When I finished my conference interpreting Master's in 2021, I had only one interpreting client: the Colorado state court system, which generally uses certified interpreters before non-certified interpreters. I had no conference interpreting clients, and my only real conference interpreting experience was as a student at Glendon College, where we were required to interpret for on-campus events as part of our degree program. At that time, I honestly was not sure if or how I was going to find a significant amount of work as a conference interpreter. Pre-2020, the only U.S.-based conference interpreters I knew who had a good amount of conference work either lived in the major coastal cities in the U.S. (which I don't) or essentially lived on the road, flying from assignment to assignment and spending perhaps 200+ nights per year in hotels (which I don't want to do).

And yet, things worked out! I hate to mention the silver lining of a pandemic that killed more than a million Americans, but my first year as a freelance interpreter was greatly facilitated by the increased availability of remote interpreting work. I was referred to a couple of excellent Canadian agencies, I found some of my own U.S.-based clients, and the demand for French interpreting in general was greater than I anticipated.

One tricky decision encountered by every beginning freelancer is the balance between rates and work volume. Many beginning interpreters lack confidence in their abilities and are afraid of not having enough work, which leads them to offer or accept low rates. Add to this the fact that interpreting rates are all over the map: in a quick online search, I came across Spanish community interpreter jobs paying $17 an hour and a Spanish federal court interpreter job paying (on salary) $147,000 per year; this huge range can make it really difficult to know what to charge as a beginner.

The dilemma is that you have to start somewhere, and working is better than not working, **but** starting at low rates has a lot of disadvantages: you risk burning out, you don't have time to market to better-paying clients because you're exhausted, your acceptance of low rates may drive down rates for other interpreters, and you may feel unmotivated to do your best work at low rates. As a counterexample, I always feel that when I have a particularly challenging assignment and I think, "Am I getting paid enough to deal with this??" I want the answer to be a resounding, "Yes!"

A lot of your first year is going to be spent simply finding work and testing the waters to locate the intersection between what you are good at, what you enjoy doing, and what clients have the budget to pay for. It can be an advantage to earn a certification (such as court or medical) relatively early in your interpreting career, because this can give you access to a "captive audience" client (a client that is obligated to use you, such as a court or hospital system), where at least some of your marketing is done for you. This is how I started: I passed the Colorado state court interpreter exam before I had ever done a paid interpreting job, and as soon as I passed, all of the managing interpreters in all of the Colorado judicial districts were informed of everyone who had passed the exam. Some offered me work right away, and I was able to follow up with all the managing interpreters and generate even more work. This was an easy, low-stress way of generating an initial flow of work (the interpreting itself was not easy or low-stress, but it didn't require a lot of marketing!).

1.12 What if You're Not 22 Years Old? Are You Too Old to Do This?

I hear, with some regularity, from freelancers and aspiring freelancers who worry that they're "too old for this." Depending on the individual, "this" might mean:

- Starting a freelance business in general
- Pursuing higher-level clients
- Pursuing a new specialization or niche (i.e. transitioning from translation to interpreting or vice versa)
- Adding something like a new language to their range of services

Of course, "old" is relative. For the record, I'm 53 as of this writing. I started freelancing when I was 30, and I know freelancers who are still going strong in their 70s, and even a few in their 80s. One individual in ATA who is mentally sharper than I am is north of 85. But still, this "too old" thing keeps cropping up.

Main Question: Does Your Brain Still Work?

This sounds laughable, but I include it here for perspective. If "too old" is on your radar screen, you probably are too old to be lots of things. An Olympic gymnast. A fighter pilot. An organ transplant surgeon. But an interpreter's main asset is mental acuity. Bottom line, if your brain still works, I'm reasonably certain you'll be OK. You're not too old for this.

Secondary Point: The Time Will Pass Anyway, So You May as Well Use it Productively

I thought about this when I took up playing the lute (a pretty difficult instrument to learn to play, as it turns out!) at 42. When I asked a musician-translator-friend whether she thought I was too old to learn to play lute, she said, "Let's say you give yourself 20 years to get really good at music. You'll be 62. But guess what… with any luck, you'll be 62 someday anyway, so why not put the time to good use?" The same can be said of freelancing. Let's say you're currently 60. If you live in a developed country and are in reasonably good health, statistically you have something like an 80% chance of living at least 20 more years. I think that's long enough for a viable freelance career, definitely.

Tertiary Point: Working as a Freelancer Protects You–to a Large Extent–From Real or Perceived Age Discrimination in a Salaried Job

The "grey ceiling" is a real thing in the salaried world. Study after study has found *zero relationship* between age and job performance. But if you're over 45 (45! Not 70!), you're less likely to be hired, more likely to be laid off, and more likely to take longer than average to find a new job. If you want or need to work past the usual retirement age, that alone could be a good reason to freelance.

However...

Starting on the bottom rung of any profession requires you to hustle. When I launched my freelance business in 2002, I was determined to make it work. I really wanted to a) work from home while my daughter was little, and b) make a healthy living without moving to a major city. Failure was not an option, so I hustled. I worked nights and weekends. I sent handwritten thank you note after handwritten thank you note. I did informational interviews that led nowhere. I had coffee or lunch with anyone who seemed like a remotely promising contact. I worked for the borderline-lousy clients that other people didn't want. I spent two years in the application process for an FBI Contract Linguist position that required an hour commute each way–not to mention the polygraph test. It worked, but it was tiring. Whether you're launching your freelance business at 22 or 75, you have to be ready to hustle.

Older freelancers have to be aware of stereotypes. In our profession, you may encounter the stereotype that older freelancers are not good with technology, for example. As an older freelancer, I would advise you to become a technology guru. Be the technology expert; be the person clients and colleagues come to for help when they have problems with translation-related software. Beat that stereotype before it even gets out of the gate. Again, learning how to use technology is just learning a new skill; you can do it.

On the plus side, you can **capitalize on positive stereotypes of older freelancers.** They're out there, so exploit them. Many clients think of older freelancers as more stable and dependable, more self-aware, more patient, and less dramatic than their younger counterparts. One client even told me, "My favorite translators were all born before 1980." Hey–take it. Emphasize to your potential clients how easy it will be to work with you.

Be prepared to be **older than a lot of the people you work for.** This is one difference I've noticed since about my mid-forties. For some time, I've been older than the average entry-level employee on the client side. In recent years, I've moved to another level. Example: I work at a co-working office, and I've noticed that when one of the office twentysomethings gives me a recommendation for something–a movie, a restaurant, a place to buy jeans–it's from their compendium of "stuff old people like." Realistically, this puts a different spin on your marketing efforts. About a year and a half ago, I lost a major direct client when they hired an in-house translator. For the first time in a long time, I actively looked for work. And I'll be honest; the age thing was a little weird. Hustling for work from people six or seven years older than my own daughter was a new experience–an experience that ultimately worked out and resulted in some excellent new clients, but one that took a bit of a mindset shift on my part.

If You're Panicking About the "Too Old" Question, I Recommend That You:

- Try not to panic. Seriously, if your brain still works, you'll be OK.

- Try not to compulsively make a big deal about your age. People who see you or talk to you will have a vague sense of how old you are. That's fine; you don't need to belabor it with a steady stream of "When I was your age..." and "Back in the typewriter era..." remarks.

- Be aware that as you get older, everyone else looks younger. Those people who look like they're 12 are actually 27 and in a position to give you work.

- Become a technology expert if you're not one already. That will go a long way toward defeating any clients' concerns about working with you.

- Embrace the fact that you are probably more self-aware, more patient, less sensitive, and more reliable than you were when you were 22. I know I sure am.

- Bonus tip: When clients think you've been freelancing for 30 years because you're over 50, take it. A friend of mine went back to school in her early 50s for a totally different career. She had mostly thought of the downsides–how many working years would she have left once she finished? But in the end, there was an upside: people automatically assumed she was a seasoned expert since she had grey hair. Again: take it, and make the most of it.

CHAPTER 2:

Deciding What to Charge

Now, let's talk about how to decide what to charge for your interpreting services. In some cases, you have no choice about what to charge because your rates are set by the entity using your services. Most court systems and many hospital systems have fixed rates; in many cases, you can even look them up online and know ahead of time what you will be paid.

When you work for agencies, they may tell you how much they pay, or it may be up to you to give a quote, and most direct clients will simply ask what you charge. Rates are a significant source of stress and fear, for beginning and experienced freelancers alike. We often fear that if we charge too much, we won't have enough work, but if we charge too little, we won't make enough money. Meanwhile, clients, particularly agencies, are (understandably) trying to get the best value for their money; it's a complicated situation.

I think the most important factor in deciding what to charge is to know ahead of time how much you need to charge in order to earn the amount of money that you need or want. This allows you to confidently turn down work that doesn't meet your target rates. This sounds simple, but it's not. As a beginner, there will probably be time (and perhaps a lot of the time!) you'd like to be working, but you don't have work. You may be balancing various types of work with various advantages and disadvantages. For example, the Colorado Judicial Branch, as of this writing, pays certified French interpreters $65 an hour with a two-hour minimum; they are my current lowest-paying client, but they have a lot of advantages as a client: they sent me 110 days of work in 2023; most of the assignments I get from them are remote hearings lasting 30 minutes or less, which frees me up to do other things if an assignment ends early; I enjoy the work and find it meaningful and fulfilling; court work is a lot less seasonal than conference work, so it can provide a good source of work during the winter and summer slow season. So, although my conference interpreting work generally pays closer to $100 an hour (I never charge by the hour for conference work, but it often boils down to approximately this hourly rate), it's not always just about the money.

Many interpreters are not numbers people, but some simple calculations can really help you get a better idea of how much you need to charge. Knowing those numbers is the first step: maybe you're not "there" right now, in terms of skills, work volume, or client base. But having a clear goal is a starting point. Here's where to start:

- **Calculate the total monthly cost of running your business:** Add up how much money you want or need in your personal bank account to cover your personal expenses each month. Think of this as your salary. To that, add every business expense that you pay for. Start with mandatory things like taxes, including self-employment tax. To that, add other financial things: a monthly amount to put into your retirement account; health insurance, if you pay for that; a monthly amount to put into your paid vacation fund so that you can afford to take time off. Then add all your "discretionary" business expenses, divided into a monthly amount: professional development, association dues (these are paid yearly, but divide them into a monthly amount), accounting services, subscription-based software, computer hardware (again, budget for this on a monthly basis even though you don't buy it each month), work-related child care, website hosting, internet service, phone service, office supplies. **Add it all up:** All of the money you need to make every month in order to keep your business running. **You may want to do this for three scenarios:**

1. Bare-bones: the absolute minimum that you can survive on, where you are either cutting back on all of your extra expenses, or taking money out of savings to fund your extra expenses

2. Mid-range: you are basically breaking even, not cutting back/taking money out of savings, but not putting money into savings and not spending much if anything on extra expenses.

3. Ideal: Where you have the same level of financial security as someone with a salaried job. **This gives you one number: the monthly cost of running your business.** For purposes of illustration, let's say that you came up with $7,000 per month, which equals $84,000 per year (this is gross income).

- **Then comes the more nuanced part.** You need to figure out how many hours per month you are likely to **generate income**, not just how many hours you are going to work. It's easy to think "40-hour work week," but most freelancers do not generate income 40 hours a week. In addition to the above-mentioned "time you'd like to be working, but don't have work," there are many tasks that clients don't pay you to do: reading and answering e-mail, preparing for assignments, following up on inquiries, marketing, professional development, coordinating with other interpreters about assignments, attending conferences, and so on. **It's probably safest to assume that you can spend 25-35 hours per week generating income.** Probably closer to 25 hours if you work with direct clients, and perhaps closer to 35 if you work with courts or agencies. **Preparation time is a huge variable here.** For something like court work, sometimes no preparation is even possible, because you may be given very little information about the case. For conference assignments, I've spent up to three hours preparing for a one-hour assignment. But let's use 25 billable hours per week to start out with, and let's say that, between vacation and holidays, you're going to take five weeks per year off, so you're going to work 47 weeks.

- **This means that you have 47 weeks** to generate $84,000, meaning $1,787 per week. And you're planning on billing 25 hours per week, so you need to charge $71.48 per hour in order to reach that target income.

- **This is meant as a guideline only.** This doesn't mean that you have to immediately start turning down every assignment that pays less than $71.48 per hour. For example, my target income is about $105 per hour, 25 hours per week, yet I work a lot for the Colorado court system, which pays $65 an hour, because I balance that out with higher-paying work, and because the majority of these court assignments take much less than two hours. The point is that you need to know, at least approximately, how much you need to charge in order to reach your financial goals.

2.1: Gold, Green, Yellow, and Red Zone Rates

Now that you know the hourly rate you need to charge in order to reach your target income, let's talk about rate zones. One way to reach your target income is to always charge the hourly rate that you calculated in the section above. For example, if I turned down every interpreting job paying less than $105 per hour, I would definitely reach my target income. However, the reality of freelance interpreting is more complicated. You are going to have assignments that pay a lower hourly rate but require less preparation, and assignments that pay a higher hourly rate but require a lot more work. For example, when I accept a court assignment, there is generally not much preparation to do (sometimes it's actually not possible to prepare, because the interpreter is given only the defendant's name and the case number), and I know there is a good chance that the assignment, for which I get paid a two-hour minimum, will last 30 minutes or less. On the flip side, I recently did a conference interpreting assignment where I did three hours of preparation for a one-hour assignment (not a typo), and we are generally required to log on 30 minutes ahead of time for remote conference assignments; so, although I was paid $525 for this "one-hour assignment," my hourly rate was more like $116.

I prefer using the idea of rate zones rather than rigidly sticking with one rate. Here's how these zones work. We'll first look at green, yellow, and red; then the gold zone.

To Start With the Simplest Zone: The Red Zone is the Rate Below Which You Never Work

For me, this would be $65/hour with a two-hour minimum. Anything below this is my red zone: a rate that I automatically turn down. Your red zone number will be different, but the point is you need to have a red zone rather than accepting whatever clients seem willing to pay, whether or not it meets your financial goals.

On the Other End of the Scale is the Green Zone: Your Ideal Rate

This is a rate that closely matches the rate you calculated in the "Deciding what to charge" section above. For example, we calculated a target hourly rate of $71.48, which might mean that your green zone is $70-$75 per hour. The green zone means you are working at a rate that meets your financial goals. It neither exceeds your financial goals nor falls short.

The Yellow Zone is a Rate That You Sometimes Work at, Often for Non-Economic Reasons

For me, this is where court interpreting falls: court interpreting does not meet my target hourly rate, but I enjoy it for other reasons. I like the work and I think it's important; and court systems are easy clients to work with because they tend to have very straightforward processes and they always pay on time. You might pursue yellow zone work because it's particularly interesting, because it's morally positive, because it furthers one of your professional goals, or for other reasons. **The main thing with yellow zone work is to not get stuck there.** It's fine to have some percentage of your work that doesn't meet your target hourly rate, but if you're working in that zone all the time, you won't be making enough money.

Then There's the All-Important Gold Zone

Particularly if you have yellow zone clients who you like working with, you may need some work in the gold zone: a rate that exceeds your target rate. For me, some of my conference interpreting work fits this bill: I do some business interpreting jobs that are very straightforward, do not require a ton of preparation, and pay well. A lot of my teaching and training work is in the gold zone as well. Much of the work that I do for law firms is in the gold zone, because law firms are often more concerned with saving time than with saving money.

Only you can decide how much time to allocate to these various zones, but even doing these calculations will help you start deciding which interpreting jobs to accept and which to turn down.

CHAPTER 3

Specifics of the Interpreting Business

3.1: What Does it Take to Become an Interpreter?

The pre-requisites to launching an interpreting career or an interpreting business really depend on where you're located and the type of work you want to do. Most importantly, you need excellent language skills. You'll have your native (A) language, or, in some cases, two native languages ("double A"), and then you'll need at least one other language: probably at least one B language, but if you work in the European market, potentially multiple C languages instead. If you work on the U.S./North American market, you're most likely to have one or more B languages that you interpret both from and into. Your skills in your B language(s) need to be very, very solid. Do not call yourself a "double A" (an interpreter with two native languages) unless you really are one, which generally means that you grew up speaking both languages interchangeably. Your B language skills need to be near-native: as close as you can get to being a native speaker without being one. By definition, C language skills are passive only, since you don't interpret into your C language.

Once you have language skills, you have a good start, but then you need interpreting skills, and to think about what kind of interpreting you want to do and whether you want to work remotely, in person, or both. Developing your interpreting skills is a lot of work; for some ideas, see this book's section on improving your interpreting skills.

3.2: Is a Graduate Degree in Interpreting Worthwhile?

Is it worthwhile to pursue a master's degree in interpreting? The answer is a resounding, "it depends!" It depends on what kind of interpreting you want to do, what your options for graduate programs are, and what your financial resources are.

Having earned a Master of Conference Interpreting (MCI) myself, I'm very glad I did, and I think that for aspiring conference interpreters, an MCI or the equivalent is well worth pursuing if a program is available for your language pair. An MCI program will help you hone your consecutive and simultaneous interpreting skills, you'll learn techniques for interpreting many different subjects and situations, and you'll make contacts that may give you a valuable networking edge once you're out on the market. I also felt that earning a conference interpreting Master's increased my confidence in my own abilities (or decreased my impostor syndrome, depending on how you want to put it) in a way that I couldn't have achieved on my own. If you're really committed to conference interpreting, I would recommend a Master's program that is:

- A full Master's in conference interpreting, not a combined Master's in translation and interpreting

- A degree that meets the criteria for the AIIC (International Association of Conference Interpreters) Schools Directory (click the "Students" tab at aiic.org)

If you're going to invest the time and money in a graduate interpreting degree and you want to be a conference interpreter, I think that a high-quality program is worth pursuing. More than in other interpreting disciplines, and certainly more than in the translation world, a conference interpreting Master's tends to be somewhat of a filter when it comes to conference interpreting. Some clients will only work with interpreters who have a conference interpreting Master's. "Where did you go to interpreting school?" is a much more common question than "Where did you study translation?" In harsh terms, many, many, translators in the U.S. are primarily or completely self-taught, and it doesn't seem to be much of a barrier to finding work, as long as your translation skills are good. In the conference interpreting world, it's much more common for interpreters to be stratified by whether they have a conference interpreting Master's.

The challenge, particularly if you live in the U.S., is finding a program and deciding how you're going to pay for it. For example, when I looked at conference interpreting Master's programs in North America, there were only four options that offered French: Middlebury Institute of International Studies at Monterey, the University of Maryland, the University of Ottawa, and Glendon College. Many conference interpreting Master's programs are two years but allow you to take an advanced entry exam to do the program in one year. Conference interpreting Master's programs also vary greatly in price depending on whether you choose a public or private university, whether you move there, and whether the program is in-person, online, or hybrid.

Yet another option is to pursue a conference interpreting Master's in another country. Programs in Europe are a lot more plentiful and a lot less expensive, but the cost of living in a city like Geneva or Paris can outweigh what you're saving in tuition, and you typically cannot work while on a student visa. If you're interested in a conference interpreting Master's, it's worth starting with the AIIC directory and looking at the options in the countries that offer your language(s), then talking to people who did those programs and getting their impressions.

If you want to be a court, medical, educational, or community interpreter, an interpreting Master's will definitely increase your skill level, but (as compared to conference interpreting) it's less clear whether it will give you a leg up in the market. It certainly never hurts to devote yourself to studying interpreting for one or two years, but if your goal is to increase your marketability/ employability or your income, you want to make sure that a degree program is going to do that.

3.3: Non-Degree Training Programs for Interpreters

Whether or not you're interested in a graduate degree in interpreting, there are lots of non-degree programs out there to choose from. You can look at programs, courses, or trainers who specialize in the kind of interpreting you want to do and take it from there. For example, when I decided in 2017 that I wanted to study for the Colorado court interpreter certification exam, I first did individual consulting with Athena Matilsky (athenasky-interpreting.com), then I purchased The Interpreter's Edge (acebo. myshopify.com), a home study course for court interpreting; then I did Interpretrain's consecutive note-taking course (interpretrain.

com). After passing the court interpreter exam, I took the Cambridge Conference Interpreting Course (cciconline.net), a two-week summer intensive that is typically held in person in Cambridge, England but was online that year (2020), and the year after I graduated from the Glendon MCI, I did CoLab (colabinterpreting.com), a one-week summer intensive in person at Glendon in Toronto. In addition, I took some webinars and short courses through Sophie Llewellyn Smith's company, The Interpreting Coach (theinterpretingcoach.com), and the American Translators Association (atanet.org). There are tons of interpreter training options out there. A few that you might want to look at are:

- Acebo/The Interpreter's Edge (acebo.myshopify.com)
- The American Translators Association (atanet.org)
- Athena Sky Interpreting (athenaskyinterpreting.com)
- De La Mora Interpreting (delamorainstitute.com)
- Bridging the Gap (various entities offer this training; search online for options)
- The Cambridge Conference Interpreting Course (cciconline.net)
- CoLab (colabinterpreting.com)
- The Community Interpreter (thecommunityinterpreter.com)
- The Interpreting Coach (theinterpretingcoach.com)
- NAJIT, the National Association of Judiciary Interpreters and Translators (najit.org)
- The University of Arizona Agnese Haury Institute (nci.arizona.edu)

3.4: Why Do Some Freelance Interpreters Fail?

Failure isn't a fun thing to contemplate, but I think it can be helpful to look at some of the reasons why freelance interpreters fail. In my opinion and experience, there are a few factors:

- The top reason for freelance interpreter failure is probably the combination of a lack of business skills and the inability or unwillingness to do enough marketing to cultivate a base of steady clients. Many interpreters are really good at the language aspects of their job, but are much less good at finding and retaining clients, negotiating rates, billing, etc. No matter how much you dislike the non-interpreting aspects of being a freelancer, the only alternative is to find an in-house job. Many freelancers (of all stripes, not just interpreters) expect much too great a return from much too little marketing effort. I often remind beginning interpreters that when I started out as a freelancer (doing exclusively translation) in 2002, I applied to over 400 translation companies during my first year in business, and it still took about 18 months until I had a steady flow of work. After I graduated from the Glendon College Master of Conference Interpreting program, the marketing aspect was a lot easier and I had a lot more freelance experience, but it still took about a year and a half until I had as much conference interpreting work as I wanted.

- Realistically, there are also interpreters whose language skills are not up to the job, thus they struggle to find and/ or retain clients. As I've mentioned before, earning an interpreter certification, particularly court or medical, is a good way to land some clients right at the start of your freelance business. It's impossible to pass these exams without excellent language skills, and I think every working interpreter has a story of working with someone who simply should not have been doing the job. Interpreters in this category tend not to last long on the market.

- Another category of struggling interpreters is those who have trouble committing to a niche and try to be all things to all clients. In some smaller languages, this may be necessary. But if you do a language where there is a good amount of work, you need to focus on work that you enjoy and are good at. For example, I do not do patient-facing medical interpreting at all. I don't enjoy it, I'm not trained for it, and thus I turn down all such assignments. Accepting anything and everything is unlikely to win you loyal, long-term clients.

3.5: How to Improve Your Spoken Language Skills

When I started pursuing interpreting, I first had to work on my spoken language skills, because I spoke so slowly in French that I couldn't even shadow regular-speed speakers. As a reminder, shadowing is the most basic skill related to simultaneous interpreting, where you repeat after the speaker in the same language; like simultaneous interpreting without the interpreting. To get my French speaking skills up to speed (literally!), I did a few things:

- Worked with French conversation teachers on italki.com, a platform that pairs live, professional teachers with language students
- Listened to French for at least an hour a day
- Read out loud in French as much as I could

- Shadowed YouTube videos of slow speakers, or slowed videos down to 0.75 speed (you can do this in the settings of most YouTube videos)

All of these techniques together really helped me. If you need to improve your language skills before you start interpreting, I highly recommend the book *Maintaining Your Second Language* by Eve Bodeux (bodeuxinternational.com/books/). The techniques I've listed above are just a few of the literally hundreds she offers on how to maintain or improve your non-native language skills. If you, like me, live in a place where you have no contact with your B language(s) in your daily life, it's a challenge to maintain your skills, but even 15-30 minutes a day can make a big difference.

3.6: How to Improve Your Interpreting Skills

There are entire books written on this topic, by interpreters much more skilled than myself. In fact, whether or not you want to be a conference interpreter (as opposed to a different specialization), I would highly recommend purchasing Andrew Gillies' *Conference Interpreting: A Student's Practice Book*, which contains more interpreting practice exercises than you can do in a lifetime.

I also highly recommend working with an interpreting coach if you can afford to do so. For some suggestions, see this book's section on non-degree training programs for interpreters. Particularly if you're preparing for a certification or accreditation exam, working with a good trainer who has passed that exam is a huge advantage. Following are some of my favorite practice techniques for improving your interpreting skills on your own. For specific tips on how to prepare for and pass an interpreting exam, see the section below this one.

Record Yourself!

- Listening to recordings of yourself interpreting, especially recordings of yourself interpreting poorly, is excruciating. It's also how you improve. Particularly if you have vocal tics such as "ummmmm," "uhhhhhhh," or clicking your tongue on your teeth or on the roof of your mouth, you probably don't even notice or hear these things when you're interpreting live, but they'll jump out at you on a recording. Recordings are also the best way to assess your delivery: pacing, intonation, and other factors you don't notice when you're interpreting. Make a practice of recording yourself during every practice session and going over the recordings carefully (painful, but necessary).

Shadow

- I think that shadowing (as a reminder: repeating after the speaker in the same language, like simultaneous interpreting without the interpreting) is a very under-used and under-valued practice technique. Shadowing helps with pacing and intonation, your actual pronunciation of words, your interpreting endurance, and your expression. When I first started learning simul, I spoke so slowly in French that I could barely shadow; shadowing is how I got up to speed (literally and figuratively) to the point that I could learn actual simul.

Don't Discount Sight Translation

- Sight translation (interpreting from a written document in another language) appears on court interpreting tests, but not in many other places. Even if you're not going to be tested on sight translation, it's a great way to improve various skills: thinking ahead, speaking more smoothly, talking around words you don't know.

Focus Sometimes on Getting Through it, and Sometimes on Perfection

- In some interpreting situations, the only way through it is through it. You just have to dive in and try and have the courage to be terrible; with consistent practice, things will get better. And sometimes you need to focus on perfection, or as close to perfection as you can get. From my music teacher I learned a practice method called "three times perfect." Pick a short section of a speech, maybe 30 seconds or so. Interpret it until you can do it three times in a row with no mistakes and with no behaviors like "ummm," "uhhhh," etc. Every time you make a mistake (or say "um," or click your tongue, or whatever you're trying not to do), start over at zero. Keep doing this until you can get through three renditions with no mistakes.

- For simul, **deliberately practice with very short and very long decalage (lag)**. Decalage, or the amount of time you lag behind the speaker during a simul rendition, is a subject of a lot of stress and debate among interpreters. Stick too close, and you risk having to completely rephrase what you're saying when the speaker changes course. Lag too far behind, and you risk forgetting what the speaker said. Everyone has a natural tendency: mine is to stick too close to the speaker, because I'm afraid of falling behind. Force yourself to periodically practice the opposite of your natural tendency; you can set an actual timer for this. For example, if you're a close-talker, set your phone timer and force yourself to wait five seconds after the speaker starts talking before you start interpreting. If you tend to lag behind, force yourself to start within two seconds of the speaker.

Learn Consecutive Symbols, to the Extent That They Work for You

- I started out hating consecutive interpreting. In court, if someone said more than about a sentence and a half without pausing, my stomach would be in knots, and I would literally be thinking, "Shut up...please stop talking NOW." These days, I honestly really like consecutive interpreting, and some of my favorite interpreting work this year has been long consecutive interpreting interviews for individuals who might talk for two to three minutes at a time. When I interpret in court, I actually prefer if people give their entire answer to a question rather than, "Your honor, I disagree, because..." "Well, because..." However, I have also come to accept that interpreting symbols are not hugely helpful to me. I definitely have a range of symbols I use regularly for common verbs (say, hear, go, return, etc.), nouns (house, man, woman, child, world, etc.), and concepts (putting an x in front of a word to negate it; underlining a word once for emphasis and more than once for extreme emphasis, so the expression "I really, really didn't like it," could be the word "like" underlined multiple times with an x in front of it). Symbols definitely save time, and I also use symbols specific to the situation: in a court case about breaking and entering, I might use "b+e," for example. And yet...I have come to accept that I am just not a hard-core symbols person because I'm not very visual. I have a hard time learning symbols in the first place, then a hard time remembering to use them, and then a hard time remembering what they mean. And yet my consecutive interpreting is accurate, and I enjoy it. I've passed three exams with consecutive interpreting sections, so I've come to accept that I'm just never going to be one of those people whose consecutive notes are mostly symbols.

Listen to a Lot of Audio Material in the Language You're Trying to Improve.

- Particularly in the run-up to my interpreting exams, it helped me a lot to simply flood my brain with French: I listened to French podcasts while I was exercising, washing the dishes, driving--pretty much any time I wasn't doing anything else. Particularly if you're more of an auditory learner, this can really help to improve your flow, pacing, vocabulary, intonation, and many other things.

3.7: How I Prepared for (and Passed on the First Try!) the State-Level Court Interpreter Exam

After a year and a half of studying, I passed the Colorado court interpreter certification exam for French in June of 2019. It was really challenging, but I passed on the first try after a lot of preparation. How much preparation? **About 400 hours of direct studying for the oral exam (plus about 20 hours for the written)** using the Acebo home study course *The Interpreter's Edge* (they don't have a language-specific version for French, so I used the Generic Edition), private coaching with interpreter trainer Athena Matilsky, and finally the practice test from the National Center for State Courts (again, no language-specific version for French, so I used the English version). On top of those 400 hours, I did an additional 100ish hours of "other" practice: French shadowing, studying flash cards of legal terms, etc. etc. In total, I probably put in about 1,000 hours of preparation for the exam.

Many People Fail the Court Interpreter Certification Exams Because:

- The test is hard
- Many people underestimate the test and don't prepare adequately
- If you do a language other than Spanish (LOTS: Language Other Than Spanish), there are very few language-specific prep materials available

However, **it is possible to prepare so that you have a reasonable chance of passing on the first try. If that's all you wanted to know**, you're good–you can stop here. If you want the details, read on!

In the Beginning

When I started freelancing in the early aughts, I did a bit of community interpreting and loved it. However, at a certain point, scheduling around my daughter's part-time preschool schedule got too complicated. So, I stopped and did only written translation from about 2004 on. But I always missed interpreting and thought (and thought and thought and thought, without taking any action...stop me if this sounds familiar) about getting back into it.

At the 2017 ATA conference, I went to Athena Matilsky's presentation on consecutive interpreting and something within me snapped. I thought, "You never have to pursue interpreting, but if you want to, it needs to be now." **So I did.** I first paid Athena for a consulting session to tell me if this idea was totally nuts (her take: maybe a little, but doable), and then I sought her advice on how to proceed. We jointly decided that I should pursue the state-level court interpreter exam, because there is a language-specific exam for French, and because–at least in Colorado–you do not have to pass all of the exam's three sections (sight translation, consecutive interpreting, simultaneous interpreting) in one shot. Within a certain period of time, you can re-take only the section that you failed. I also surmised that there might be a reasonable local market for French interpreting since there was, at that time, only one court-certified French interpreter in the whole state.

I dusted off my long-dormant copy of The Interpreter's Edge and got to work, trying to practice for about 30-60 minutes, five times a week. I then met with Athena about twice a month to do live interpreting practice sessions with her critiquing my performance. Operation Interpreter was rolling.

The Orientation and Written Exam

I'll give a huge shoutout to the Colorado Judicial Branch for the organization of their interpreter recruitment and training system. The process is very straightforward:

- **Attend a full-day orientation**
- **Take the written exam**
- **If you pass the written exam, take the oral exam**

The orientation is simply a matter of attending; as long as you are there for the full day (the cost varies, but I think mine was $150), you are eligible for the written exam. The orientation covers the requirements for working in the Colorado courts, interpreter ethics, and the qualification or certification process, plus specific information on preparing for each component of the exam.

The written exam is–depending on where you were educated and your level of knowledge of the legal system–**either not that big of a deal, or really hard.** As an educated native English speaker with some knowledge of the U.S. legal system, I didn't find it extremely challenging; I passed with a score in the 90s after preparing for about 20 hours. Mostly, I studied flashcards of all the legal terms in the guide Colorado Judicial provided. However, if I had to take a corresponding test on the French or Swiss legal systems, the test would have been extremely challenging. I think that how much you need to prepare really depends on your baseline language skills and knowledge of the U.S. legal system.

The Major Challenge: the Oral Exam

After passing the written exam, the next step was the oral, **which was by far my biggest challenge in the whole process.** If you live in a state that uses the National Center for State Courts' exam, the test consists of:

- Sight translation in both directions (from and into English)
- A consecutive interpreting dialogue where you interpret in both directions (i.e. one actor plays a court official who speaks English and the other plays a witness or defendant who doesn't, and you interpret for both)
- A simultaneous interpreting passage where you interpret from English into your other language

As I mentioned above, I used The Interpreter's Edge for all my English into French preparation. The major challenge was finding materials for French into English. If you do a LOTS language, I would highly recommend working with a trainer for your language if you can find someone. Trainers often have some of their own materials they've paid to develop or know where to point you to find resources for your language. To be honest, I was never able to find a good source of English<>French consecutive interpreting dialogues where you have speakers of both languages in the same passage. So I mostly used things like French Canadian court videos on YouTube, French court documents, etc. to practice going into English.

Pro Tips for Preparing for the Oral

Here's a lightning round of my top tips for preparing for the oral:

Do Every Passage in *The Interpreter's Edge* Multiple Times

- As Athena told me, continue working on each passage until either it's perfect or you're ready to throw the book out the window. This really helped me. Rather than thinking, "Well, that was awful!" (which most of my renditions were when I first started out), I would record myself, listen to the recording, analyze what I did wrong, and then repeat the passage until it got better.

Know All the Boilerplate Legal Stuff Like the Back of Your Hand

- When you go to the exam, you are dealing with a lot of unknowns. Mostly, you have no idea what the subject matter of your case will be. It could be anything from armed robbery to traffic court to attempted murder. However, you can be sure that certain boilerplate legal language appears in every case: words like judge, jury, verdict, plea. Phrases like "ladies and gentlemen of the jury," "raise your right hand to be sworn in." And even whole utterances like, "Do you swear to tell the truth, the whole truth, and nothing but the truth." You do not want to be racking your brain for the French word for "witness stand" (*la barre des témoins*) when there's a 90% chance the term will appear somewhere on the test. Make flashcards of as many of those types of terms as you can think of and go over them again, and again, and again. I actually kept my flashcards in a little Ziploc bag so I could study them at breakfast, on the bus, while waiting on a conference call, etc., etc. Knowing those terms inside and out really helped my confidence level when I went into the exam.

When You Make a Mistake in Simultaneous, Don't Let it Derail You

- I think many people fail the simultaneous section because they get rattled by a word that they know they got wrong. Instead of missing just that one word, they pause to think about it (*oh no…the number was 70 and I said 17*) and miss the rest of the sentence, resulting in multiple error points. It's really, really, really hard to do, but when you miss a word in simultaneous, just let it float away like a balloon and keep on interpreting. A tip from one of my music teachers, "As soon as you hear the mistake, it's already over; let it go and worry later about why it happened."

Use Your Two Consecutive Repetitions, but Use Them Judiciously

- Consecutive is by far my weakest mode (working on it still…), so I really wanted to take advantage of the option to have two of the consecutive segments repeated. I think most states offer this; you just tell the tester, "Repeat that please," and they'll play the segment again; you can request that for two segments. On the exam, I got very lucky in that I selected the two longest segments for my repetitions, but that is a hard call when you're very nervous: you don't want to waste your repetitions on short, easy segments, but you also don't want to leave a repetition unused.

Focus on Passing the Test, Not on Being Perfect

- This is a really hard one if you–like 99% of language professionals–are a perfectionist. To pass the exam in Colorado, I had to get a 70% on all three sections. But I didn't want to get a 70; I wanted to get a 100. It took time to accept that that wasn't going to happen, and that I needed to focus on the requirements for passing, not on perfection. It can also be somewhat terrifying to realize that–as difficult as the exam is–interpreting in the real world is even harder. For example, the simultaneous passage on the exam is 125 words per minute. In real life, very few people talk that slowly. People also do not politely pause at the end of a thought while you take notes. In a real court hearing, you don't get two repetitions. Just keep reminding yourself that **right at this moment, you don't need to worry about that.** The simultaneous passage is 125 words a minute, you get pauses and repetitions during the consecutive, and your goal is to pass the exam.

The Big Moment: Exam Day

Before registering for the oral exam, I took the NCSC practice exam and scored above an 80% on all sections, going only from English into French (my weaker direction). I figured (hoped/ prayed) that I had a good chance of getting above a 70 on the real test even with the nervousness factor, so I registered for the April sitting in Denver. Athena gave me great advice for the final tune-up: finish on a high note. **Two to three days before the exam, do a passage very well, then stop.** Don't be preparing until the 11th hour–you won't improve, you'll just make yourself more nervous. So that's what I did: I picked a fast simultaneous passage from The Interpreter's Edge that I had actually cried over (no exaggeration) the first time I tried to interpret it (as in "I'll never be able to do this"), did it solidly, then put the prep materials on the shelf.

The day of the exam, **I arrived an hour early to the testing location** so I wouldn't be stressed out about the time, and listened to French music on my phone while I waited. This helped get my French-language juices flowing without the pressure of having to interpret.

The court staff member who administered my exam was great. She was very calm and confident about administering the test, which really helped. A few notes from the actual sitting:

- **The tester may sit at the same table as you,** almost close enough to touch you. So you might want to practice with another person (your spouse, a friend, etc.) sitting at the table with you while you interpret so you're used to that.

- **There is often a time limit for the sight and consecutive sections,** so make sure you've practiced doing those modes efficiently (not pausing for too long) so that you'll finish within the time limit.

- **I was allowed to use headphones for the simultaneous but not for the consecutive.** Again, I would practice this at home so you're used to it.

After my exam, I felt that it went about how I expected. That sounds kind of anticlimactic, but I also felt it was a sign that I had prepared thoroughly. As I expected, sight translation was my highest score, then simultaneous, then (the dreaded) consecutive, but I passed all three sections on the first try, which I was excited about.

Parting Thoughts

If you're interested in taking the state-level court exam, I would definitely encourage you to go for it, but be realistic about the amount of preparation it requires and what skills you need to practice in order to pass.

Since passing the exam, I've seen a number of benefits: court interpreting work of course, plus, oddly enough, I've gotten a lot more translation work from law firms, who want someone certified for both court interpreting and translation. I'm not sure I see the logic there, but if it's a business advantage, great. Passing the exam has also given me the motivation to start preparing for the Department of State interpreting exams, as a "someday" goal!

3.8: My Experience in the Glendon College Master of Conference Interpreting Program

During the 2020-2021 academic year (at the height of COVID), I completed a Master of Conference Interpreting (MCI) degree fully online (the Canadian border was closed for that entire time, so there was no possibility of going in person) from Glendon College, the French-speaking campus of York University in Toronto, Canada.

Doing an MCI had been a longtime dream for me, but I could never figure out how to make it work logistically. I wanted to do a program on the "approved schools" list of AIIC, the International Association of Conference Interpreters, and there are only four programs in North America that offer an English<>French MCI, none of which are anywhere near where I live. Before online school was a thing, I just couldn't figure out how to handle the logistics and finances of doing this. But during the pandemic, most of the major MCI programs went online, and the first year of the Glendon program had always been online, so they had experience with how to run a fully remote program. I made a snap decision to apply to the program; I found out about it only in July when I did the Cambridge Conference Interpreting Course (also fully remote). Then I took the advanced entry exams that allow you to do the program in one year, was accepted, and started the program at the beginning of September.

I really enjoyed the Glendon program, and it was an incredible opportunity to do a full Master's, just in conference interpreting, without having to relocate. Online education has its pluses and minuses, but I felt that Glendon did a good job with it, and because there was absolutely nothing else to do during the COVID lockdowns, I was able to really devote myself to the program while still working part-time.

A Day in the Life...

In the French language group, we had about 13 hours a week of live classes (the Glendon program really emphasizes the live aspect versus watching a bunch of recordings, which I liked), plus our cohort had an interpreting technology intensive class in addition to our regular classes. I found this load manageable (most classes were two hours, and we had one day a week with no classes) and as the semester went on, I found a better balance between attending classes, doing my own practice sessions, and practicing with other people from the French group. I really tried to attend every class (only missed one class, one time, each semester!) and do at least one practice session a week with someone else in the French group, plus multiple practice sessions on my own.

I found that by putting in 10-12 hour days, things felt manageable, even though I was still working part-time. That sounds like a lot, but...there was a pandemic on...so I also had a lot more time on my hands than I normally would. I hate working from home, but not working from home was a lot more complicated during COVID. The co-working office where I was working until March 14, 2020, closed down, and I worked from home for a very unproductive six months. Then, in September, I found a small, private office with its own ventilation system, about a 10-minute walk from my house. It was a very isolating time for the whole world, but the setup worked for me.

I typically got to my office around 7:45 AM because classes often started at 8, and I got into a little routine of meditating for five minutes before the day started. Another small but important sanity routine is that I love (like, really love) coffee and I hate chugging it quickly in the morning, so I took my coffee with me to my office. So pretty much five days a week, I would drink my coffee while looking out the beautiful glass door in my office, meditate for five minutes, then go straight through with classes and work until around 6 PM (taking a short break to run or do yoga at lunch), then do maybe an hour or two more at home in the evening. It was an intense time, but it felt doable.

How Did All of This Work Online?

Online school plus work can definitely be a lot of screen time. At one point, I was having major problems with eye strain, so I took a couple of weeks where I forced myself to do non-screen things (read a physical magazine or book, play music, exercise) in the evening. That helped a lot.

A big advantage of the York/Glendon program is that Year 1 of the MCI program (which I did not do because I took the advanced entry exam to go directly into Year 2) has been online since the program's inception almost ten years ago. It's definitely an advantage to be in a program that has the online methods dialed in, even though my year was their first doing Year 2 online. It would definitely have been great to be on campus, and Glendon has since transitioned to a hybrid model where students are in-person for about three stints per year. Glendon has an amazing interpreting lab and I would have loved to be working in person with the instructors and the other French students, but I felt like fully online was not a bad Plan B at all. As a bonus, we learned **a lot** about remote interpreting, which proved incredibly useful. At that time (now more than four years ago), I think we all assumed in-person work would come roaring back after the height of COVID, but in my case, that has proven not to be true. Pretty much all of my conference interpreting work (~100 days per year) is remote, and I find that the option to do remote interpreting now means clients are reluctant to pay travel, hotel, and per diem. Much of my Canadian work now involves in-person events where only the interpreters are remote, which I wouldn't have anticipated in 2020.

What We actually Did in the MCI Program

I keep making this comparison, but getting better at interpreting is a lot like getting better at playing a musical instrument. There's some theory, and there's lots, and lots, and lots of practice. Practice on different types of subject matter: everything from colony collapse disorder to tension between France and Germany and how that affects the value of the euro. Practice on different types of speakers: people who talk fast, people who talk slowly, people with heavy accents, people with circuitous speaking styles. Practice with panel discussions and question and answer sessions. Just lots and lots of practice.

We also had the chance to interpret for lots of live events at York University, which was an aspect of the Glendon program that I found very useful. Again, these could be anything: I did two Town Hall meetings, one on the COVID situation and one on York's new campus; staff meetings; seminars for the Year 1 interpreting students; an information session for prospective students in the MCI program…lots of different stuff. The York staffers were always very appreciative of our work, and it was a great opportunity to practice in a real-life situation.

A Few Surprises

Someone asked me the other day whether anything about the Glendon program or doing a Master's in conference interpreting surprised me. Why yes, thanks for asking:

- I never really believed that most of the magic behind interpreting is, like the magic behind playing a musical instrument, just lots and lots of practice. It's really more of a skill than a talent. People have varying levels of talent, but the first time Yo-Yo Ma picked up a cello, he didn't sight-read the Bach cello suites. The same is true of conference interpreting: *no one* is good at simultaneous interpreting without first learning the techniques and practicing them for lots of hours. *No one* is good at taking notes on a long consecutive speech without learning the techniques and practicing them over and over again. But the beauty of this is that you *definitely can* become good at things that initially seem like magical powers. Case in point: Back when I was still learning the very basics of interpreting to prepare for the Colorado French court interpreter exam, I overheard two very experienced conference interpreters talking about long consecutive interpreting. One said, "Once you've learned the techniques to do a 10-minute speech, you can easily do 20 minutes." The other replied, "Oh, definitely, no problem there." And my reaction, as I struggled in the trenches of doing *30-second segments* to prepare for the court interpreter exam, was something along the lines of, "WHAAAAAAAAAAAAT???" But guess what--now I actually agree completely. At the end of our last semester, one of my classmates and I did a practice session with a 10-minute consecutive speech, and we agreed it really wasn't that bad. It wasn't a super technical, fast, or complex speech, but we took notes for 10 minutes and then interpreted it back, and it really went OK. That felt like progress. I've gone from (literally) feeling my stomach churning when someone in a court hearing talks for more than a minute to actually encouraging people to keep on talking so that I get more of the whole idea.

- This is a little weird to say, but the acceptance of self-taught interpreters on the U.S. market (where many, many interpreters have little to no formal training) used to not bother me at all. It still doesn't, because the reality is that we have huge interpreting needs but very few training programs, especially outside the most-spoken languages. However, I do see now that trained interpreters really are much better at the job. That's not earthshaking news, but I now see it with my own eyes--or, rather, hear it with my own ears. I'm not sure what the solution is, because there are so many issues: the U.S. population speaks about 430 languages; many interpreters, especially at the community level, simply don't earn enough money to make extensive training a viable option; many interpreting clients don't see the value of a trained professional interpreter; etc., etc. But still, this is worth noting: Formal training makes a huge difference.

How Second Semester Went

At the start of the academic year, we had some hope that Canada would open up to international students and we'd be able to be on campus at Glendon for the January-April term, but COVID had other plans, so we remained online. Second semester included the same classes we took during first semester, interspersed with some really great intensive courses with Helen Campbell, Michelle Hof, and Andy Gillies, which added a lot to our experience. As in the first semester, we also had the opportunity to interpret for many live events at Glendon, including a lot of conferences and seminars for Black History Month. Otherwise, things were much the same as during the first half of the year: I kept working part time doing translation, teaching online courses, and doing a little court interpreting, but the workload was manageable because there still was not much else to do during COVID.

The Exit Exam Process

Classes ended in mid-April and then we had about six weeks to focus on preparing for our exit exams. These are high-stakes because at Glendon, as in most AIIC-listed conference interpreting programs, you don't get the degree until/unless you pass the exit exams, no matter how you've done in the classes. I did the degree in English (A) and French (B), so I had four exit exams: a six-minute consecutive and a 12-minute simultaneous in both directions. Although Glendon offers retake opportunities, my goal was to pass all four exams on the first try so I could just get the degree and move on with actually finding conference interpreting work.

I do best with a lot of structure, so I developed a simple practice routine and set a goal of going through that routine every single day, knowing that if I aimed for seven days a week, I'd actually probably do six days. I got this tip from Athena Matilsky when I worked with her to prepare for the Colorado Court interpreter exam. My routine was:

- Listen to French news (usually France 24 or France Culture) for around 15 minutes
- Practice numbers on the website Numerizer for around 15 minutes
- Interpret one consecutive speech, alternating days between English and French
- Interpret one simultaneous speech, alternating days between English and French

This took around an hour, and I found that removing the analysis paralysis of deciding what to practice was really helpful. Instead of focusing on the best or optimal practice for that day, I just did the same sequence of exercises over and over again. I also practiced with other students from my program so that we could give each other feedback, which was also very helpful.

Exit Exam Week

We took our exams from home, using a platform called GoReact. I liked GoReact a lot because it plays the source video and records you at the same time, so that you don't have to worry about running multiple platforms. We were able to practice with GoReact a bunch of times so that we wouldn't be stressed about how to operate it on exam day, which helped a lot. I decided to control absolutely everything I could during exam week because I wanted to feel that if I didn't pass, it was purely because my skills weren't up to the standard that the evaluation jury expected, not because I was underprepared or because I didn't have my exam-taking environment set up properly. My husband had the opportunity to go out of town and I encouraged him to go so that I would have the house to myself and be able to be on my own schedule. The night before my first exam, I went to a two-hour yoga class with live harp music and went straight to bed when I got home. A few other tips that our instructors and fellow students gave me that really helped:

- Make a checklist so you don't sit down on exam day and realize that you don't have a pen, or that your notebook is out of pages, or whatever. Include seemingly obvious things like getting a drink of water and going to the bathroom 10 minutes before the start time. This sounds really basic, but I wanted to set everything up with as little left to chance as possible, because I knew I would be nervous on the day of the exam.

- Rather than focusing on giving a Carnegie Hall performance on exam day (which you probably won't do because you'll be nervous), focus on using the prep period to improve your overall skill level so that if you do, let's say, 80% of your best on exam day, it's still good enough to pass.

- Whatever happens on exam day, don't stop once you've started a speech. If you have an internet glitch, or think it's the wrong speech, or miss an entire sentence, or whatever, just keep going, because there's still a chance you will pass, but if you stop in the middle of the speech, you will definitely fail.

My first set of exams was English into French (which was good for me, because it's my harder direction and I got it over with first), then we had a rest day, then French into English. In the end I thought that the exam speeches were about what I expected: neither significantly easier nor significantly harder than I anticipated. I felt very drained afterward from the tension and anticipation, but I also felt that I had done a solid performance, and if I failed, there really was nothing to do except study more and try again.

But I passed! I was prepared to retake any exams that I had failed, but it's also a relief to have successfully completed the program and be able to move on to looking for work. And if you too are harboring a big, crazy dream, go for it! It's not too late, but someday it will be, and the time is going to pass anyway, so get going!

3.9: My First Year as a Conference Interpreter

When I did the Glendon program, I honestly wasn't sure what I was going to do with an MCI degree. At the time, the only people I knew who did a significant amount of conference interpreting work did so by either living in a major city or living in hotels 200+ nights per year, neither of which is appealing to me. There's very little conference interpreting work where I live, but I thought (correctly, it turns out) that it would be crazy not to take advantage of doing an MCI remotely while I could. When I finished the Glendon program, my only interpreting client was the Colorado court system, which is obligated to use certified interpreters when they're available, so I had done no (literally zero) marketing of my interpreting services. I wasn't really sure what would come of the MCI degree!

It turns out that remote interpreting has become fully embedded in the business landscape, and I did the MCI at an opportune time. In addition, having a degree from a Canadian interpreting school opened a lot of doors in the Canadian market, where French interpreting is a big deal and very in-demand. Following are some notes I assembled after my first full year of conference interpreting; I think it's interesting to return to them and remember what worked out as planned and what was different!

In that first year, my conference interpreting work volume was **about what I expected:** it took a while to build up, and I'd say that conference interpreting is more networking and referral-based than cold marketing-based. But I'm happy with the quantity, type, and quality of work that I have, and I love the actual interpreting work even more than I thought I would. Overall, I'm very happy with the decision to do a conference interpreting Master's and with this new career direction; I would count the Glendon program as one of the best career decisions I ever made, and possibly the best.

I had originally set a goal to have my work volume be **half translation and half interpreting** within one to two years of graduating from the Glendon program, and that did happen. In 2021, I switched from Excel sheets to QuickBooks Online for accounting (a painful but ultimately very worthwhile process), so it's easy to see where my income is coming from. In the first five months of 2022, the amount I earned from interpreting for agencies almost equaled the amount I earned translating for direct clients, and it's an amount I'm happy with. By 2024, this trend continued, and I now do about 70% interpreting and 30% translation.

I feel like **the Glendon program prepared me really well for the real world of conference interpreting.** I think that doing an AIIC-level conference interpreting program makes a huge difference in one's interpreting skill and confidence and is well worth the time and money. And here, you heard me say it: a couple of my favorite assignments this year involved long consecutive, which was the source of at least one sobbing breakdown during the program. If you're learning long consecutive, stick with it!

I have lots of observations about the differences between translation and interpreting, but here's a major one: I think **it could be challenging** to launch a freelance interpreting business if you're not already self-employed or if you don't have a flexible schedule. In my experience, most beginning freelance translators launch their businesses by working another job alongside their translation work until they have enough freelance work to cut the cord. I think that could be harder (not impossible, but harder) with interpreting. As a newbie, a lot of clients are going to start you with work that is less desirable, schedule wise: the classic example being a one-hour assignment in the middle of the day, or things that start early or end late, or "The other interpreter is having a power outage, can you start NOW?" I actually enjoy those kinds of assignments because I'm already self-employed anyway, but it's something to consider if you're making the leap from another job.

On the other hand, I think that interpreting, and particularly conference interpreting, **can become economically viable** faster than a fledgling translation business generally does. In most cases, a minimum charge conference interpreting job is going to pay a lot more (perhaps 10x more) than a minimum charge translation job because most conference interpreting work is going to be billed by the half day or full day rather than by the minute or hour. When I first started translating, a lot of my translation work was minimum charge jobs paying less than $100, and it takes a lot of those types of jobs to add up to a full-time income.

3.10: Preparing for and Passing an Interpreter Certification or Credentialing Exam

This is a huge topic, one that could easily be the topic of its own book (an idea for the future!). Whether you do court, medical, or conference interpreting, there's a good chance that you'll have to take a high-stakes exam at some point in your career. While I am far from the world's best interpreter, as of this writing I've taken three high-stakes exams (the Colorado state court interpreter certification exam, the exit exams for the Glendon College Master of Conference Interpreting program, and the exams administered by SOSi, the company that currently provides interpreters to U.S. immigration courts). I passed all these exams on the first try, so I feel like my exam preparation strategy is a solid one.

3.11: Why Do so Many Interpreters Fail Certification Exams?

An important starting point is knowing that *lots of interpreters fail exams*. Whether it's a state court exam or the E.U. interpreter accreditation exams, lots of people fail. I think there are three main reasons for this:

1. Interpreting exams are hard; most exams have a passing rate ranging from 5-20%, and some sources say that the pass rates for the U.S. Federal Court Interpreter Exam may be even lower.

2. Perhaps most critically, people don't adequately prepare for interpreting exams, or they prepare in ways that are not effective.

3. Exam day is nerve-racking, and people approach exam day with the wrong mindset (and, again, don't adequately prepare).

I think that the most important keys to success are:

- It takes *a lot of time* (typically in the hundreds of hours) to adequately prepare for an interpreting exam.

- Consistency (practicing five to six days a week, every single week) is key.

- You want to focus more on raising the overall level of your interpreting skills (so that, say, 80% of your best is good enough to pass on exam day) rather than on delivering the interpreting performance of your life on exam day (you probably won't!).

- You want to control what you can control, leaving absolutely nothing to chance on exam day.

- You have to practice with materials that are more difficult than what you think will be on the exam so that you develop strategies for speakers who are fast, who deliver dense material, or who are hard to understand.

3.12: How Long Does it Take to Prepare for an Interpreting Exam?

Everyone is different, and it depends on how much progress you need to make. If you're starting from zero, you may need to work on your interpreting skills *and* your language skills. This was the case for me when I started preparing for the Colorado state court interpreter exams in early 2018. I could barely shadow (repeat after the speaker in the same language) in French, much less interpret, and I had pretty much zero note-taking skills for consecutive. I studied for this exam for about a year and a half, doing approximately 400 hours of direct preparation for the exam, and an equal or greater number of hours working on my spoken French, so probably close to 1,000 hours total (and I passed the consecutive by one point, so I could not have done any less prep!).

When I did the Glendon Master of Conference Interpreting program, the program lasted one academic year, and then I did about three months of preparation for the exams, practicing an hour a day, five to six days a week, for the first six weeks, and two to three hours a day, five to six days a week, for the second six weeks. However you slice it, it takes a lot of time to prep for an interpreting exam!

3.13: How to Create a Training Plan for an Interpreting Exam

The heart of any exam prep strategy is a training plan: a simple, repeatable practice routine with components that you can switch in and switch out, depending on the components of your exam. Part of what you're trying to do is train your brain to think that what you'll have to do on the exam is not that big of a deal, just something you've done many, many times before--so you want to create as iron-clad a routine as possible. For example, when I prepared for the Glendon College exit exams, the most stressful component (for me) was the consecutive speeches where we had to listen to a five to seven minute speech while taking notes, then interpret into French or English. One of my "calming" strategies was to always introduce my consecutive rendition in the same way: "I'll start my speech now," for English, and "Je vais commencer mon discours," for French.

Your daily practice sessions should have three components:

1. A warm-up (more on this below)

2. A short block of time to work on something challenging that you know will be on the exam (more on this below)

3. A solid block of time actually interpreting, aligned with the sections of your exam.

It is extremely important to understand the components of your exam before you begin practicing. I can't stress this enough and I can't tell you how many people don't know this. For example, on many U.S. court interpreting exams, the simultaneous portion is only from English into your other language (because you would rarely, if ever, do simul into English in court, since only the defendant is listening to you when you do simul). The consecutive portion of some interpreting exams is a bilingual dialogue, while on other exams it's a monolingual speech. It's really, really important to know this before you start.

3.14: The Sections of Your Practice Session

As mentioned above, your practice sessions should have four components. Each practice session should last around 45-60 minutes, unless there's a particular reason that you need to go longer or shorter.

- Warm up: The point here is just to get your brain moving. If one of your languages is clearly your weaker one, focus the warm up on that. My go-to warm up was to either shadow a French news show or just listen to it. This had the added advantage of helping me keep up with current events in the French-speaking world. Spend 10-15 minutes on this.

- Next, spend 10-15 minutes on very focused practice of an interpreting skill that is hard for you and that will definitely be on the exam. For me, this was numbers. Every interpreting exam on earth includes numbers, and in my experience, numbers are a lot easier to get better at versus other difficult things (jokes, idioms, quotations) that are on a lot of interpreting exams. I used Numerizer (numerizer. pro) for this and highly recommend it. But you can do anything you want with this section: if your main struggle is eliminating "um" and "uh" from your delivery, work on that. If your main struggle is falling behind the speaker, work on that.

- Then you want to spend about 30 minutes working on actual interpreting in a way that aligns with the sections of your exam. When I prepared for the Colorado state court interpreter exams, I used The Interpreter's Edge (acebo. myshopify.com) almost exclusively, working through each section in order. When I prepared for the Glendon College exit exams, I mirrored the exam structure: one consecutive speech and one simultaneous speech, alternating directions (English to French or French to English) daily.

3.15: Other Practice Techniques to Add to Your Sessions

If you're looking to mix things up, here are some things to consider adding to your practice sessions, regardless of the type of exam you're preparing for:

- Record yourself! Recording yourself and listening to the recording, preferably with a transcript of what you interpreted, is both excruciating (even listening to the sound of your own voice can be cringe-inducing at first, let alone evaluating your own interpreting performance) and critical. You have to do it and either evaluate the recordings yourself, or have them evaluated by an interpreting coach or colleague.

- Whether or not your exam includes consecutive interpreting, practice long consecutive interpreting *without notes*. This is a key skill for any interpreter because it trains your brain to listen instead of freaking out when there's no way that you can get every detail. Particularly if you're doing conference interpreting and one of your challenges is to focus on the message rather than the words (this is something I'm always working on), you should definitely practice this. Listen to a five to seven-minute speech and then interpret as much as you can, as if you were simply telling a story: stay calm, stay expressive, and just tell the listener the core message of what you heard.

- Three times perfect: I got this technique from my music teacher! Perfect interpreting almost never happens, but this is a good way to break bad habits such as "um," "uh," and other problematic voice behaviors. Interpreting is really stressful, and lots of interpreters do weird things with their mouths and voices; sometimes those behaviors become so ingrained that we don't even realize we're doing them. Mine used to be tongue-clicking: when I paused during a rendition and started talking again, I would click my tongue against my upper teeth, and it was audible on the microphone, a major problem. Here's what you do: pick a short (30-60 seconds) passage and interpret it over and over, until you do it three times in a row with no mistakes. Every time you make a mistake, the counter resets; so if you do it perfectly twice and then make a mistake on the third rendition, you restart at zero. This method really helped me break my tongue-clicking habit, and it can be very helpful for any problematic behavior you're trying to eliminate.

3.16: Additional Practice Material and Techniques

Following are a few other resources you might want to use:

- The slow down/speed up feature on YouTube. This is available for most YouTube videos by clicking Settings (gear icon) on the video. When I started learning simul, I couldn't even shadow French at full speed, so I slowed the videos down to .75 speed. If you're practicing for a particularly challenging exam, you could speed up the videos.

- As mentioned above, Acebo's The Interpreter's Edge is pretty much the gold standard for court interpreting exam prep in the U.S.; you definitely need it if that's the type of exam you're preparing for.

- Another great resource for court interpreting exams are court reporter YouTube channels. Court reporters are obsessed with words per minute and practice using court transcripts read out at various speeds, which are excellent resources for court interpreters. I used the Humphreys University Court Reporting channel (@ humphreysuniversitycourtre6729 on YouTube) a lot when I was studying for the court interpreter exam.

- The European Union Speech Repository (speech-repository. webcloud.ec.europa.eu) is a key resource for conference interpreting practice. It contains speeches at all levels (from beginner to very advanced) for consecutive and simultaneous on a wide variety of topics; you can also choose between prepared speeches and actual recorded EU meeting material.

- You should also find the authoritative public broadcasting outlet for your source and target languages: In the U.S. I listen to a lot of NPR (National Public Radio), and for French I use either France Culture or France 24.

3.17: Practice Tests

Sadly, many people do not make use of the practice tests that are available for the interpreting test they are going to take. Practice tests are an underused resource *that can give you an example of what the test will actually consist of!!* You should take any and all practice tests available for your exam; look on the testing entity's website or ask them directly about practice tests.

You want to take the practice test under the same conditions as the actual exam (timing, available resources, repetitions, headphones, etc.). There is a lot of variation in exam structures: whether all of the exam sections go in both directions, or only one; whether or not you can use headphones; whether or not you can ask for repetitions of consecutive segments, etc. Make sure you fully understand this before the day of the test.

If your exam is scored numerically (i.e., you are scored purely on accuracy, which is the case for many court interpreting exams), you also want to score your practice exam, or ask a colleague to score it, using the same standards as the real exam. In my case, exam-day nerves deducted about 10 percentage points from my performance on all sections of the court exam, so you don't want to count on passing the real exam if you barely passed the practice exam.

3.18: My Exam Prep Mindset

In the run-up to all three high-stakes interpreting exams I've taken, I told myself this: If I fail this exam because my interpreting isn't good enough, I can accept that, and I'll look at what went wrong, prepare more, and take the test again. If I fail this exam because I didn't prepare enough, I can't accept that: I absolutely will not let myself under-prepare and fail.

Andrew Clifford, the director of the Glendon College conference interpreting program, gave me one of the best prep tips I've ever gotten: Do not focus your prep on doing the best interpreting performance of your life on exam day. The reality is, you're probably not going to. The focus of your prep should be to *raise the overall level of your interpreting* so that about 80% of your best is still good enough to pass. This tip served me really well because it removed a lot of the stress over trying to do a perfect performance on exam day.

3.19: The Day of Your Exam

Prepping for the day of your exam actually begins the day before. Around 24 hours before your exam, you want to do your final practice session: pick something you know you can interpret well, do it, and then you're done. Don't practice right before your exam because it's unlikely to improve your skills (what's done is done!) and will only make you more nervous if you make any mistakes. The night before my conference interpreting exams, I went to a two-hour yoga class, then went home and immediately went to bed!

On the day of the exam, *leave nothing to chance.* Lots of things you cannot control are going to be thrown at you (such as the content of the exam), so you want to control absolutely everything that you can. If you're taking the exam from home, set everything up (including extra notebooks, pens, water bottle, etc.) just the way you want it, well in advance of the exam. If you're taking the exam at a testing center, make sure you have everything you need with you (see if the entity offering the exam has a list of what you can and can't bring) and arrive at the testing center well in advance of the test. If you have to drive more than about an hour to the test location, consider getting a hotel within walking distance of the testing center.

Here's the key thing you want to tell yourself on the day of the test: This doesn't have to be the best interpreting performance of your entire life. You just have to do what you've already done hundreds of times (because of all those practice sessions!): a solid job with no major mistakes.

3.20: The Snowball Effect

From talking to many interpreters who have passed and failed interpreting exams, I think that people mainly fail exams for two reasons: lack of proper preparation, and the snowball effect. Lack of preparation speaks for itself, and the snowball effect is what tends to result in well-prepared interpreters failing an exam. Here's what happens:

- The interpreter is well-prepared and has an appropriate skill level for the exam

- A "curveball" comes, perhaps at the very beginning of the exam. For example, the opening statement in a court simultaneous passage might be, "The defendant is here today to be arraigned on charges of grand larceny…" and the interpreter thinks, "Oh no…I have no idea how to say 'grand larceny' in my language." Or, the passage includes a long list of names, or numbers, or something else that the interpreter can't get completely.

- The interpreter gets flustered, telling themselves, "This is the key term in this passage, and I don't know it! This is a disaster!" or "Six names and I only got two! I'm bombing already!"

- Things spiral downhill from there, and soon, the interpreter is floundering.

The snowball effect is real, and here's my advice on how to avoid it:

1. Practice with materials that are too hard or too technical for your current level; speed up the audio if you have to. Practice with speakers who have heavy accents, who talk really fast. This helps you develop coping strategies for when you know you're not getting everything, rather than falling into the trap of interpreting the first half of one sentence, trailing off into nowhere, and then interpreting the second half of the next sentence.

2. Remember that really good interpreters make it through entire interpretations where they don't know or can't

understand one of the key concepts: it's not ideal, but it's possible.

3. Practice reformulating complicated concepts and talking around words you don't know. In the "grand larceny" example above, the interpreter could have simply said, "The defendant is here today to be arraigned on various charges." That's missing a key element, but it is clear and it conveys the messages of defendant-arraignment-charges. The interpreter would undoubtedly lose some points, but perhaps the snowball effect could be avoided. Likewise with the list of names: if the speaker rattles off, "We'd like to thank today's speakers, Dr. X, Dr. Y, and Dr. Z," the interpreter could simply say, "We'd like to thank the doctors who will be speaking today." Again, it's not 100% accurate, but it's not a disaster and it leaves the interpreter ready to do a better job on the next sentence.

3.21: What if You Fail?

If you follow all of the tips in this section of the book, I think there's an excellent chance that you will pass whatever exam you're preparing for. However, well-prepared and highly skilled interpreters do still fail exams. In that case, I think it's important to:

- Give yourself time to feel whatever you feel: mad, sad, the test was unfair, you know what you did wrong, you don't know what you did wrong--just whatever you feel.

- Decide whether you want to take the exam again or not. Both options are OK. I've talked to interpreters who took the state court exam three or four times before they finally passed. And I've talked to interpreters who failed the oral portion of the federal court interpreter exam twice, and said, "I'm done, I don't need to put myself through that again, and there's plenty of other work out there."

- If you decide that you want to take the exam again, I think it's a good idea to start thinking about the timeline fairly soon, since some exams are only offered once a year or even less often, and you don't want to miss the window of opportunity to retake the exam.

- Then make a plan, focusing on what went wrong the first time, and what you need to do differently now.

3.22: Who Do Interpreters Work for?

Freelance interpreters work for a huge range of clients, but it can be overwhelming to think of every possible client who might need you, whether you're qualified to work for them, and how you might go about obtaining work from them. Instead, let's start by looking at four main types of clients: interpreting agencies, direct clients, court systems, and government entities/international organizations.

3.23: Working for Agencies

Many interpreters get the bulk of their work from interpreting agencies. These agencies could be general—covering a wide range of interpreting services—or specialized—covering only health-care interpreting, or conference interpreting, for example. Like any type of client, agencies have advantages and disadvantages. On the plus side, agencies find the end clients for you. Most interpreters would rather interpret than market, so agencies can be great clients if they like you, have interesting work, and pay well and on time. For whatever reason (I have various theories about this, but it's a topic for another day!), there has also been a lot less rate erosion in the interpreting agency market than in the translation agency market. Whether this is a question of supply and demand (people leaving the interpreting market and entering the translation market during COVID?), interpreters' own resistance to rate erosion, interpreting being perceived as a more specialized skill, all of those, or something else entirely, it's been my experience that, particularly for legal and conference interpreting, agencies still pay quite well. I enjoy working with interpreting agencies and get most of my work from them.

Additionally, if the agency is good, you just do your preparation work, then show up and interpret. The agency should be the one to make sure that the end client sends the preparation materials well ahead of time, has the proper technology setup, etc., and it's nice to have this burden off your shoulders so that you can focus on interpreting.

There are also downsides to working with agencies. Because they do all the work to find and retain the end client, the agency is going to keep a significant part of the money that the end client pays. Having the agency between you and the end client can be a plus or a minus: it's great to "just interpret," but it's also frustrating when an agency doesn't follow through on their part of the job and fails to ask the end client for the materials you need to prepare for the job. Overall, I like working for interpreting agencies, but there are definitely tradeoffs. I also find (and this may be specific to my experience) that most conference interpreting clients are inclined to go through an agency, perhaps because they are intimidated by having to find multiple interpreters, or perhaps because they want help with the technology.

It's also worth mentioning that there are other types of "agencies" that you might want to contact in addition to pure interpreting agencies. For example, I've worked for legal services agencies that find deposition interpreters for law firms. There are a/v companies that provide interpreters in addition to other services for conferences, and there are interpreting-specific tech companies that provide consulting and a/v services for remote and hybrid events. Court reporting firms are also often asked for referrals for deposition interpreters. Keep your antennae up for these other types of agencies that might be good sources of interpreting work.

3.24: Working for Direct Clients

It's also possible to work directly for interpreting clients without an agency in the middle. Businesses, law firms, government offices, consulting firms, and other entities may be interested in hiring you directly, rather than through an agency. This can work out well, in many ways: you will potentially earn more than you would through an agency, you can communicate directly with the client rather than waiting for the agency project manager to communicate on your behalf, and you can develop a personal relationship with the client that keeps them coming back to you for more assignments, rather than depending on the agency to select you when a particular end client needs an interpreter.

If you want to work with direct clients, the main difference is that you don't just show up and interpret, and you need to distinguish between working as an interpreter and working as an interpreting consultant and a/v technician, which you should not do unless you have that expertise and are compensated accordingly. In many cases, straightforward assignments can involve very little extra work: I have a couple of clients who send me consecutive interpreting assignments that are done using Zoom (without the interpreting feature) or even a telephone conference call line (remember those??). Where things get complicated is when the direct client needs remote simultaneous and has never used a remote interpreting platform; or has multiple languages; or you need to use relay and the client doesn't understand what that involves; or the client is putting on an in-person event with remote interpreters and hasn't thought about how they're going to feed the audio into the interpreting platform; or a myriad of other issues that can arise, particularly in a hybrid or remote situation where you can't simply step out of the booth and try to resolve the issue.

3.25: Working for Court Systems

In the U.S., court systems at all levels (from municipal to federal) use interpreters in a variety of languages. If you're interested in working for the courts, a good place to start is your state court system's office of language access, or the National Center for State Courts' interpreter resources page (ncsc.org/education-and-careers/state-interpreter-certification). The NCSC website has links to the language access programs in most states, so it can be a good place to start.

In most states, you need to go through some sort of registration or certification process in order to work in the courts. The requirements will typically depend on whether certification is available in your language and how much of an emphasis your state puts on certification, if it is available. In many states, it is virtually impossible for Spanish court interpreters to work in the courts without being certified. Some states have a tiered process where you can pass a written test in English about the U.S. legal system, then take a speaking test (not an interpreting test) in your non-English language, and then be classified as a "registered" interpreter (or another designation, depending on the state).

The safest option is to pass the interpreter certification exam in a state that uses the NCSC exam (formerly known as the Consortium exam). As of this writing, the NCSC oral exam is available in Amharic, Arabic, Cantonese, Tagalog, French, Haitian Creole, Hmong, Khmer, Korean, Mandarin, Polish, Portuguese, Russian, Spanish, and Vietnamese, with abbreviated exams available for Bosnian/Serbian/Croatian and Vietnamese. However, some states (notably, California and New York) do not use the NCSC exams, although they may accept a passing score on the NCSC exam and reciprocally recognize it. Here again, the best place to start is your state judicial branch's office of language access and go from there.

Working in the courts, like all interpreting settings, has its pluses and minuses. Court work is certainly needed and meaningful; some interpreters find it exciting, and some find it incredibly stressful. I personally *love* working in court and am really glad that I put in the effort to prepare for and pass my state's court interpreter exam.

Working conditions vary between states: Some states are very interpreter-friendly and will give preference to certified interpreters, offer a two to three hour minimum, and pay for travel time and mileage. Other states are more concerned with saving money than ensuring quality interpreting, and working conditions will reflect this. In most states, pay rates for court interpreters are set via a collective agreement and cannot be negotiated. It's not uncommon for LOTS (Languages Other Than Spanish) interpreters to be paid more than Spanish interpreters: where I live, in Colorado, certified LOTS interpreters are paid 18% more than certified Spanish interpreters.

Whether you will work remotely or in-person as a court interpreter depends on the jurisdictions you work for. In my area, probably 75% of our court work is still remote (this may be different for Spanish interpreters), and I also work for several neighboring states for which I do *only* remote work. However, some states have returned to primarily in-person hearings; if you prefer to work remotely, this is something to ask about when you start the court certification process.

Salaried jobs for state courts also exist, primarily for Spanish interpreters. You typically have a better shot at these jobs if you've worked as a contractor for the system you're planning on applying to.

The United States federal courts certify Spanish interpreters only, through a lengthy process that requires you to take the written exam and then wait until the next year to take the oral, if you pass the written. Rates for federal court interpreters are established via a collective agreement that covers all of the federal courts, and the federal courts hire both contract and salaried interpreters. The federal courts seem to have returned to mostly in-person hearings; if you prefer to work remotely, this is something to ask about when you start the certification process. For more information about becoming a federally certified court interpreter, see: uscourts.gov/services-forms/federal-court-interpreters/ federal-court-interpreter-certification-examination.

3.26: Working for Government Entities and International Organizations

International organizations, such as the United Nations and the UN system entities, NATO, the European Union and European Commission entities, etc., use lots of interpreters but can be challenging to break into, and some require specific language combinations. For example, as of this writing, in order to sit for the UN LCE (Language Competitive Examination), you need at least three of the UN official languages, unless you do English<>Arabic or English<>Chinese.

Many national government entities, such as the United States Department of State, take interpreters with only one language pair, and may have a lot of opportunities for freelance work. Some of these assignments may be much longer than what a typical private-sector client would offer (potentially several weeks at a time), and this can be attractive (or unattractive) depending on how much other work you have.

If you are interested in interpreting for international organizations, expect to take a test or even a series of tests. Some of these are offered in-person only, while other entities (specifically the U.S. State Department) seem to have moved to mostly online testing. Interpreting for international organizations has its pluses and minuses: if you are interested in a permanent staff position, these organizations are probably your best option, and many pay quite well. The flip side is that the application processes can be long, you may have to wait a specified amount of time if you fail the exam on the first try, and you are probably locked into the contractually negotiated rates that these organizations pay. The best option is to research the application process on the organization's website and try to talk to other interpreters who work for them to get input about their experience.

3.27: Combining Translation and Interpreting

For context, from 2002 (when I started freelancing) until 2019 (when I passed the Colorado state court interpreter exam), I was exclusively a French to English translator. From 2019 until 2021 (when I graduated from the Glendon College Master of Conference Interpreting program), my work volume was about 90% translation and 10% interpreting, particularly because court interpreting dropped to almost zero for the first few months of COVID, and I turned down most interpreting assignments during the year I was studying at Glendon.

When I finished the Glendon program, my goal was to be 50/50 translation and interpreting within a year and a half of finishing the program (meaning by the end of 2022). I thought that this was wildly optimistic because I didn't know much about the conference interpreting market, there's very little in-person conference interpreting work where I live, and I assumed (incorrectly) that most conference interpreting work was going to go back to in-person once the acute phase of the pandemic was over. In reality, interpreting work is booming: In 2023 I earned U.S. $65K from interpreting–12K from court interpreting and 53K from conference interpreting–and I did almost 200 days of interpreting (103 court assignments and 90 conference assignments). This was almost double the amount of interpreting I did in 2022, while my translation work stayed stable.

Since I finished my conference interpreting Master's, I've come to a few realizations about combining translation and interpreting:

Most importantly, I really enjoy doing equal amounts of translation and interpreting. I've heard people comment that it's relatively uncommon to really combine translation and interpreting: You're more likely to encounter interpreters who occasionally translate at times of the year when interpreting work is slow, or translators who do a small amount of court interpreting, for example. I actually really enjoy doing real amounts of both translation and interpreting, and I hope to continue this!

I find that interpreting makes me a better translator and translating makes me a better interpreter. Interpreting has taught me a lot about focusing on meaning, rather than words; using shorter, simpler ways of expressing complicated concepts; knowing when to add a little flair and when to cut out the fluff. Translation has taught me a lot about finding precisely the right word; slowing down instead of rushing; making sure that the expression is exactly what I want. I feel both skills have benefited each other.

I've also come to appreciate the advantages of both translation and interpreting. When you finish an interpreting assignment, whether it went well or poorly, it's over. Even if you were recorded (which allows you to go back and obsess over what you said!), there's no way to change it. As one of my music teachers once told me: the reason not to obsess over mistakes is that, by the time you hear them, they're already over. This is a beautiful thing about interpreting! The beautiful thing about translation is taking as long as you want (as long as you meet the deadline!) to pick just the right word. When you're interpreting, you have about a quarter of a second to contemplate the difference between the words "maybe" and "perhaps," or "careless" and "reckless." At times it can feel like being fired out of a cannon, and I've come to really appreciate the luxury of time when I'm translating.

It can also be challenging to combine the two, in terms of workflow. Because I have a good deal of interpreting work, I'm often too busy to take on last-minute, large translation projects. Translation work that blends well with interpreting is definitely somewhat of a niche market, because many translation clients want someone who is fully and immediately available. Then there are the business aspects of translation and interpreting. A few observations there:

- **Interpreting, at least the flavors of interpreting that I do (mostly remote simultaneous and court)**, is really in demand. It took me about the same amount of time (18 months) to really "launch" as translator in 2002 as I did as an interpreter in 2021, but marketing my interpreting services involved a lot less work.

- **Interesting, well-paid interpreting work tends to find me**, whereas I have to knock on a lot more doors to find interesting, well-paid translation work. I don't feel, at all, that the translation profession is dying. At the same time, **there's a much smaller pool of French conference/court interpreters** than the pool of French to English translators. Clients might want to cut corners on interpreting, but you can't really do simultaneous interpreting if you haven't studied and practiced it extensively, and automated interpreting is way behind machine translation. I lose a lot of translation work because the client finds someone cheaper; it's pretty rare for that to happen with interpreting.

- **For reasons that I keep mulling over without a clear answer**, interpreting agency rates haven't cratered in the way that translation agency rates have. I'd estimate that translation agency rates have dropped by about half in the 20+ years I've been a translator (and that's not including even lower-paid machine translation post-editing work), while I have **several interpreting agency clients that voluntarily raised their rates** in the past few years. I'm really not sure whether this is a case of increased translation automation, more freelance translators entering the market (giving an "anyone can do it" flavor to the profession), interpreters exerting pressure on other interpreters not to decrease their rates, fewer interpreters entering the market, interpreters who dropped out of the market during COVID or because they hate remote interpreting, all of these factors, none of these factors, or something else entirely.

Overall, I am very, very happy that I decided to pursue interpreting in addition to translation, and I'm happy with the mix of clients that I have right now. If you are also considering such a career pivot, I would encourage it, and I hope these tips are helpful!

3.28: Setting Your Interpreting Rates

Interpreting rates are the source of an enormous amount of stress and controversy, for new and experienced interpreters alike. There are so many sources of anxiety around rates: charging too little and not having enough work or being perceived by colleagues as undercutting them or "spoiling the market;" or charging too much and not having enough work. To add to the situation, there's the question of billing increments (per minute, per hour, per half day, per full day) and working conditions (are you paid for travel time, waiting time, overtime, and how many interpreters is the client hiring for the job).

Below is an overview of common interpreter billing increments and their pros and cons. Note that I will *not discuss billing by the minute.* I know that some clients, specifically agencies that hire interpreters for over-the-phone interpreting, do require per-minute billing, but I see this as a disrespectful, nickel-and-dime approach to billing for what should be viewed as a professional service.

3.29: Charging by the Hour

Charging by the hour is common in medical and court interpreting. In fact, entities such as state court systems may have set hourly rates for different categories of interpreters. In the court systems in my home state of Colorado, one can simply look up the hourly rate paid to:

- Non-certified Spanish interpreters
- Certified Spanish interpreters
- Non-certified interpreters in languages other than Spanish
- Certified interpreters in languages other than Spanish

Many medical interpreting clients will simply tell you that they pay X dollars per hour. This seems simple, but there are various other factors to consider, such as:

- What is the minimum billing increment? One hour? Two hours? Something else?
- Are you paid starting at the time you were requested to show up, or from the time you actually start interpreting? For example, if you're requested for a medical appointment at 10 AM but sit in the waiting room until 10:45, are you paid starting at 10:00, or at 10:45?
- After the minimum billing increment, in what increment do you bill? For example, if your client pays a two-hour minimum and your assignment ends up lasting two hours and 10 minutes, are you paid for three hours? Two and a quarter hours? Something else?

The advantage of charging by the hour is that it's a clear, simple billing increment that everyone understands. The disadvantage is that hourly billing doesn't reflect all of the other time that goes into your interpreting work: most specifically, preparation and research, but also travel and waiting, not to mention all the time it took to develop your interpreting expertise.

3.30: Charging by the Half or Full Day

Charging by the half or full day is most common in the conference interpreting world. Some other clients, such as the U.S. federal courts, also pay by the half and full day. The advantage of half and full day billing is that you avoid the hair-splitting issues mentioned in the section above, like whether an assignment that ran over by three minutes is going to be billed extra or not. Half and full day billing allows the client to simply know what the interpreting job is going to cost them, before it even starts. A few issues to consider if you bill by the half or full day:

- What constitutes a half or full day? How many hours of interpreting are included in each increment? Do the hours have to be consecutive? For example, if a client wants you to interpret from 10-12 and 2-4, is that a half day or a full day?

- What constitutes a team of interpreters (this is a working conditions issue, but is more likely to come up for half-day and full-day assignments)? Most interpreters (wisely) will not work alone on simultaneous interpreting assignments, but some interpreters and interpreting associations feel that even two interpreters are not enough for, let's say, assignments of more than four hours, and that three interpreters should be hired in that case.

- Does your half-day or full-day rate include a sound check/ tech rehearsal, if it happens on a different day than the event? Most interpreters will expect to be asked to log on (for a remote event) or show up (for an in-person event) at least 20-30 minutes before the start time. For remote or hybrid events, the client may want to do a sound check or tech rehearsal at a different time than the actual event, and you need to decide if you're going to charge an additional fee for that.

3.31: Charging for Travel Time, Mileage, Travel Expenses, and Per Diem

An additional and significant consideration is whether you're going to charge for anything other than interpreting time: specifically, for travel time, mileage, travel expenses (plane ticket, hotel, etc.), or per diem (a lump sum typically paid for travel assignments to cover meals and incidentals; Latin for "per day," and sometimes you'll see the expression "per noctem"/per night).

Here again, if your client is a court system or large hospital, setting these fees may not be up to you. The client may simply say, "Here's what we pay." As an example, the Colorado state court system pays half of the interpreting rate for travel time and the IRS standard rate for mileage, using a table that they send you when you are put on the court interpreter roster, which shows the time and distance from your home address to every court location in the state. That's a very detailed system, but you could also use something more general: "I charge X hours of travel time for anywhere in the Boston metro area," or something similar.

Interpreters who travel overnight for assignments will typically either bill the client for travel expenses or have the client book their travel and pay for it. This is an important distinction because if the assignment is cancelled (see the section below on cancellation fees) and you have already fronted out money for a plane ticket, hotel, etc., you have to really trust that the client is going to reimburse you for that in addition to paying your cancellation fee.

Per diem is typically a simpler alternative to reimbursing you for meals and incidentals on a travel assignment. Rather than having you submit receipts for every sandwich and cup of coffee, the client will often propose paying a per diem.

If you're the one setting the rates, an additional option is to roll all of these non-interpreting charges into a higher lump sum charge. This might be appealing to some clients and less appealing to others, so it's worth thinking about.

3.32: Cancellation Fees

Cancellation fees are a huge issue in the interpreting world, because assignments do get cancelled, sometimes at the last minute. Just in the past few months, I've had multiple interpreting assignments cancelled, because:

- A court case was settled at the last minute
- A court defendant didn't show up
- A conference client had technical difficulties and their meeting couldn't happen
- An agency cancelled an assignment at the last minute with no stated explanation

Interpreting assignments get cancelled for all kinds of reasons, from the mundane (the person you're supposed to interpret for forgot about the appointment and didn't show up) to the rare but significant (there's a mass shooting in the city where the conference is being held and the international delegates you were supposed to interpret for decide not to come).

Most importantly, make sure that the cancellation policy is clearly set forth in every interpreting contract you sign, and that the details are included. Rather than just stating a number of days or weeks, I prefer to clearly state the cancellation deadline for every assignment, as in, "The interpreter's full fee for this assignment, which begins at 9 AM Eastern time on Wednesday, September 13, is payable if the assignment is cancelled after 9 AM Eastern time on Wednesday, September 6." For legal assignments (for example, depositions), I also specify that the cancellation fee is payable if the party needing the interpreter does not show up or decides to speak English instead of using the interpreter.

Standard cancellation fees vary by client and even by location. In the U.S., particularly for court or medical assignments, you may see cancellation fees as short as 24 to 48 hours before the assignment, whereas the European conference interpreting sector often uses an "option" system, where the interpreter is paid in full if an assignment (even if several months in advance) is cancelled after a contract is signed. The main factor here is to have a clear cancellation policy of your own, or to understand the client's cancellation policy and get it in writing. Some clients include weekends in the cancellation period, some only include business days, some will have a caveat that, in order to be paid the cancellation fee, you have to remain available for another assignment on the date of the cancelled assignment, and all sorts of other specific clauses. Just make sure you understand them and that they are stated in writing!

3.33: Contracts and Terms of Service

Having a clear contract for every interpreting assignment is very important. If you work with agencies that have their own contracts, it is also very important to *read* those contracts before you sign them. This sounds obvious, but a lot of interpreters skip this step!

If you work with direct clients, you may need to create your own contracts. A good resource for this is the American Translators Association's model contract for interpreting services, which is available to ATA members for free. Following are a few clauses that you may need to consider when creating or signing an interpreting contract:

Payment

- This is probably the key element, although by no means the only important element, in a contract. How much are you getting paid? In what increments (half day, full day, hour, minute)? If you are getting paid by the hour or the minute, what is the minimum charge (one hour, two hours, three hours)? As a rule, conference interpreting is typically paid by the half or full day, and court, medical, educational, and community interpreting are often paid by the hour. You may see over-the-phone interpreting companies that pay by the minute (whether or not to accept this is up to you). A few considerations to think about here:

  ○ For an hourly assignment, make sure to establish: 1) The minimum number of hours for which you get paid, and 2) The increments in which you get paid after the minimum number of hours. For example, the Colorado state court system pays a two-hour minimum, and after that you're paid in 15-minute increments. So, if you interpret for two hours and one minute, you get paid for two hours and 15 minutes. But (at least as of this writing), the agency that provides interpreters to the U.S. immigration courts pays for a full hour as soon as you roll over into that hour. So, if you interpret for two hours and one minute, you're paid for three hours.

- Billing by the minute is, in my opinion, not desirable. Even if the client pays a per-minute rate that adds up to a decent hourly rate, I personally do not think it reflects a professional interpreter's required training, skills, and experience to be issuing invoices for these very small amounts.

- Overtime, for half day or full day assignments. Some clients include a short "grace period" (typically around 15 minutes), after which the interpreter gets paid overtime, typically at an hourly rate.

- Travel time. For hourly assignments that are on site, make sure to specify whether or not you are paid for travel time. You also want to specify what rate is paid for travel time (for example, the Colorado state courts pay half of your interpreting rate for travel time) and whether you are paid a predetermined amount of travel time, or your actual travel time.

- Waiting time. Same here: for court and medical assignments, ideally you want to be paid your full interpreting rate for the full time that you're on site or online. However, some clients will try to get you to agree not to be paid for waiting time; make sure you check the contract for this type of clause.

Reserved Time

- This is mostly applicable to court and medical assignments. You want to make sure that you are getting paid for the entire time that the client may need you, and that if you are reserved for two hours, it's acceptable to tell the client that you have to leave at the end of the two hours. Some clients will try to get around this by telling you that you get paid for a two-hour minimum but may be needed for up to four hours, for example. I personally will not agree to this type of clause because I feel that it's exploitative. Particularly if you work mainly for court, medical, or educational clients, you need a lot of appointments in order to earn a decent income, and it's difficult to do that if you're holding extra time for a client that doesn't end up needing it.

Cancellation Policy

- This is a huge one, because interpreting assignments get cancelled and rescheduled all the time. See this book's section on cancellation fees for more information.

Recording Fees

- Particularly in the age of remote interpreting, many assignments (both remote and on site) are recorded. You should always be informed when you're going to be recorded. Interpreters' opinions on recording fees vary: some interpreters feel that you're doing the same amount of work and, if the recording is just for the client's reference, it's not that big of a deal. Others feel that a substantial recording fee (perhaps 25%-33% on top of your regular rate) is fair, because the client can then do whatever they want with the recording: post it on YouTube, charge people to download it, etc.

Boothmate/Interpreting Partner

- This is another point where opinions vary, but the important thing is to clarify your own thinking about the length of time for which you are willing to work alone. Many state court systems only assign two interpreters if the assignment is expected to go longer than two hours. Some conference interpreters will work alone for up to an hour, while others won't work alone at all; in some countries (not typically the U.S.), it's industry standard to hire three interpreters if the assignment lasts longer than four hours. In the private sector, law firms often expect that deposition interpreters will work for two to three hours alone. It's also fine (and safer and healthier for the interpreter) to never work alone; you just have to make sure that clients know this up front and be ready to turn down assignments that don't fit your desired working conditions.

CHAPTER 4

Remote Interpreting

4.1: Love It or Hate It?

Prior to March 2020, remote interpreting existed, but as a relatively small segment of the market, and often using very simple technology such as over-the-phone (OPI) interpreting. Suddenly, remote interpreting became the norm, and something that interpreters had to either embrace or at least tolerate if they wanted to keep working at the height of COVID.

Remote interpreting brought huge changes to the interpreting market; some positive, some negative, and some in the "it depends" category. Perhaps the biggest change (whether you see it as positive or negative) was accessibility, both for clients looking to hire interpreters and for interpreters seeking work. In the pre-COVID era, some types of interpreting, particularly conference interpreting, required interpreters to either live in or near a major city or be willing to travel extensively. It wasn't unusual for busy conference interpreters to spend 200+ days on the road, and it also wasn't unusual for interpreters to cut back or cease interpreting if they had location or travel constraints. All of a sudden, an interpreter with significant family responsibilities had a lot more options. At the same time, accessibility comes with some caveats. The fact that an interpreter with an internet connection and a headset could start marketing their services to clients all over the world led to somewhat of an "anyone can do it" phenomenon, something that has existed in the translation world for a long time but took longer to appear in the interpreting world. Likewise, clients suddenly had a wider range of interpreters from which to choose. Clients also didn't have the barrier of having to pay for interpreters' travel and lodging, which motivated some to start using interpreters for the first time.

Some interpreters feel neutral about remote work: they don't love it, but they don't hate it. Others feel that the in-person aspect of the job *is* the job: seeing the venue, talking to the speakers, getting the feel of the event they're interpreting for. Still others love the flexibility and options that remote interpreting offers and the fact that remote interpreting involves more actual interpreting and less travel, schmoozing with clients, etc.

One objective reality of remote interpreting is that it shifts a lot of responsibility from the client to the interpreter in terms of technology and the physical interpreting location. Instead of showing up at a venue and perhaps bringing their own headphones, interpreters now must worry about having not only a robust remote interpreting setup but also backup systems. Not all clients have or are willing to hire an a/v technician, instead assigning an employee to manage remote interpreting, which means that a lot of the onus for good sound (incoming and outgoing) is on the interpreters. Many clients expect that remote interpreting will cost less than in-person, when often the opposite is true (or should be true) due to the expenses interpreters incur for setting up and maintaining a home interpreting studio. Interpreting hubs, centralized locations where interpreters would work remotely with the assistance of a technician and client-provided hardware, surged in popularity during COVID, but now seem to be on the wane, probably due to the expense and hassle of maintaining them.

Whether you love it or hate it, remote interpreting is likely to remain a significant part of the interpreting market, especially now that interpreters have become used to working from home and clients have become used to not paying to bring interpreters on site. In the next section, we'll look at how to set up a good remote interpreting studio.

4.2: Setting Up a Home Interpreting Studio

How much time and money to spend setting up a home interpreting studio depends on your resources (material and financial) and how much remote interpreting you're planning on doing. A basic home interpreting studio should include:

- A soundproof or at least very quiet location without noise from roads, pets, children, loud HVAC systems, etc.

- A robust internet connection, using wired ethernet rather than wi-fi if at all possible

- A fast, reliable computer

- At least two good headsets or headset/microphone setups: a headset or microphone is a significant single point of failure, so you want at least two (see the next section for information on choosing a headset)

- A second device for connecting with an interpreting partner and, possibly, a third device for taking relay (less common now that platforms like Zoom are adding relay features, but still good to have)

- A good desk and chair that are comfortable to sit at for long periods

Then, "nice to have" (or perhaps critical, depending on your location and how reliable your internet and power are), would be:

- A second internet connection with a second provider, to be used if your main internet connection goes down

- A backup power system, such as a UPS, in case your power goes out

- An attractive background or virtual background and good lighting, if the client wants you to appear on video (this is often the case with court interpreting)

4.3: Choosing a Headset or Microphone, and a Bit About Acoustic Shock

Your headset and/or microphone are one of the most critical pieces of equipment in your remote interpreting studio. If you want to get a group of interpreters shouting at each other, start talking about headset and microphone preferences; it's a very personal decision and one that interpreters have very intense feelings about.

In the pre-COVID era, interpreters who worked exclusively on-site were responsible only for their own headphones, and even those were sometimes provided by the client. Interpreting booths always included fixed microphones that the interpreter would speak into, so the interpreter's only responsibility was incoming sound. In the remote world, you're responsible for both the incoming and the outgoing sound, which is a much bigger responsibility.

Fortunately, good headsets and microphones have come down a lot in price, and there are a lot of options to choose from. The first decision is whether you want a headset that includes headphones and a microphone, or a pair of headphones and a standalone microphone. Personally, I prefer an all-in-one headset because it's convenient, doesn't require sitting a fixed distance from the microphone, can be used on a single USB or audio jack connection, and is easy to carry while traveling. Many interpreters feel the opposite and think they get better incoming and outgoing sound quality from headphones with a standalone microphone.

Regardless of which option you choose, you want to consider:

- Comfort; you're going to be wearing your headphones or headset for many hours at a time.

- On-ear, in-ear, or over-ear design. On-ear (typically involving circular foam pads that sit on the outside of your ears) is the most common design and the one featured on most headsets. On-ear headphones usually have average to good incoming sound quality and also allow you to hear your own voice while you're talking. In-ear is more commonly seen in earbuds, which interpreters don't typically use unless they're using a second device to listen to relay, but some interpreters who use standalone microphones do use high-end in-ear headphones, such as those made by Bang and Olafson. In-ear headphones avoid the headband required by on-ear and over-ear designs, and thus can be quite light and comfortable. Over-ear headphones are most commonly used by audiophiles and gamers and are designed to have excellent incoming sound quality and to be very comfortable. The catch for an interpreter is that you need open-back or semi-open back over-ear headphones so that you can hear yourself, otherwise you may get into the habit of removing one earphone, which can lead to turning up the incoming volume and damaging your hearing.

Whatever type of headphones you choose, you want to make sure that they are comfortable for long periods of time, that they fit your head, and that they have some form of acoustic shock protection, meaning that they automatically limit the incoming sound to a specific number of decibels. Acoustic shock is a serious risk for all interpreters, but particularly for those who work remotely without a technician to manage their incoming sound. Acoustic shock can result from a single incident, such as a speaker dropping a live microphone or a sudden blast of feedback into the incoming audio feed. However, in the RSI (remote simultaneous interpreting) world, the greater risk is the cumulative effects of chronic bad audio. When faced with a speaker who isn't using a microphone, or who has a lot of background noise, or a spotty internet connection, you can really only do three things: stop interpreting completely; interpret only what you can hear, possibly resulting in an interpretation that your listeners can't make sense of; or turn up the incoming audio feed to get more of the useful sound, but also more of the distortion. Over time, this can have a serious effect on your hearing, and acoustic shock is likely to become a major problem for interpreters who work primarily or exclusively online. To protect yourself as much as possible, always use a headset with acoustic shock protection and, to whatever extent you can, insist on interpreting only for speakers who are using headsets or standalone microphones, not their integrated laptop microphones.

I own two Sennheiser headsets, the SC65 and the SC75 (the technical specifications are the same, only the cosmetic features are different). These headsets have acoustic shock protection, have good incoming and outgoing sound quality, are not very expensive (under U.S. $60), and are approved by most of the major remote interpreting platforms. It's definitely worth doing your own research, but I would recommend the Sennheiser SC65 or SC75 if you want a reliable option that isn't extremely expensive. I also have an AudioTechnica open-back gaming headset that I really like. It was around U.S. $120 and I like the over-ear fit slightly better than the Sennheiser headsets, and the microphone is more adjustable, but it's too large to easily take with me on work-related trips where I only want to take one bag. Finally, I have a standalone microphone—the Shure MV7+--which has incredible sound quality (I use it to record my podcast, Training for Translators) but, because it's on a boom arm and has to be positioned directly in front of my mouth and thus obscures a good bit of my face, it's not great for remote court interpreting where I have to have my video on while I'm interpreting.

Headsets and microphones are a really personal choice, and if you do a lot of remote interpreting, you're going to spend a lot of time listening through your headphones and talking into your microphone. You definitely want to read reviews of various set-ups and try them if possible. For example, I love the sound quality from the microphones on Jabra headsets; the sound is crisp but warm, and I love interpreting for people who are speaking into Jabra headset mics. However, when I tried a Jabra myself, the earphones didn't fit me at all (they felt like plastic muffins smashing my ears), so it's a good idea to try a few brands and see what you think.

4.4: Remote Interpreting Platforms

At the beginning of the pandemic, a variety of platforms sprang up to support remote simultaneous interpreting. These platforms offered a variety of features: some allowed you to see, hear, and/or message your boothmate; some allowed relay interpreting (where an interpreter can listen to, and interpret from, another interpreter's audio output rather than from the main floor speaker); some had handover assistance features (see the next section for more on handovers in remote interpreting).

Over time, it seems that, at least in the U.S. conference interpreting market, many of these fuller-featured platforms have fallen out of use, and most clients simply use Zoom or Webex. Many interpreters comment that clients simply don't see the need for these platforms, don't want to learn to use them, and don't want to pay for them, especially when the interpreting features included in Zoom have gotten more robust over time (for example, Zoom now allows relay interpreting; you can listen to another language's interpreting output channel, then broadcast your interpretation over your language's channel). Many government clients use Webex for security reasons, but its simultaneous interpreting features are just being rolled out as of this writing, so it often requires the use of a separate phone line for simultaneous interpreting.

If you do remote simultaneous interpreting, it is important to understand how remote interpreting platforms work, and it is also the reality, at least in the U.S. private market, that the vast majority of clients just use Zoom, which is a pretty simple platform to learn to use.

4.5: Handovers in Remote Interpreting

One thing that remains tricky in remote interpreting is handovers, when one interpreter "hands" the microphone over to their partner. When you're interpreting in person, handovers are not much of an issue because you can see the other interpreter. Typically, interpreters will decide on a "shift" length, typically 20-30 minutes, then use some sort of hand signal for the actual switch. In remote interpreting, this is a lot harder, because the interpreters may not even be in the same country, much less the same room. Following are a few options for how to smoothly switch between remote interpreters.

- When you are switching interpreters, the most important thing is **to avoid having two people talking at once**. It's preferable to have a few seconds of silence, rather than both interpreters talking at the same time.

- In order to avoid this, you need a **backchannel**: a way to communicate with your virtual boothmate without the listeners being aware of this. The three main options are to set up a backchannel that allows you to see, hear, or message your boothmate.

- In the early days of remote simultaneous interpreting, **many interpreters were (understandably) very nervous about these remote handovers and opted for a really robust backchannel**, such as a WhatsApp or FaceTime video and audio call, that allowed you to see and hear your boothmate. This minimizes the risk of a sloppy handover (with two people talking at once or a long period of silence), but it can also be really distracting (when you're already trying to watch the main Zoom screen, the meeting materials, and possibly a reference document or glossary), it requires another device that has to be charged and running, and it consumes internet bandwidth.

- There are now easier, leaner ways to accomplish this seeing/hearing if you'd like to do that: Whereby (whereby.com) and Cymo Booth (cymo.io) are two tools that you might want to check out.

- Over time, as interpreters have gotten more used to remote handovers, many have opted for a more slimmed-down, less distracting system, such as:

- Interpreters set up a messaging chat on a platform like WhatsApp or Signal. I prefer using WhatsApp Web because I can keep the window open on my second monitor instead of having to use my phone.

- Interpreters decide on a "shift" length (typically 20-30 minutes) before the event starts and determine which interpreter will do the first shift.

- A few minutes before the end of the first shift, the non-active interpreter sends the active interpreter a series of nudges with a reminder that the shift end time is approaching. My regular boothmates and I typically do 30-minute shifts and often do a reminder at five minutes (putting something simple like "5 mins" in the chat), followed by "2 mins," and then the all-important, "1 minute, watching your mic," or "1 minute, ready on your mute." The non-active interpreter then carefully watches the active interpreter's microphone, and when the active interpreter mutes, the non-active interpreter un-mutes and starts interpreting; handover complete.

- There are a few issues and variations with this system. Some interpreters prefer, instead of watching for the active interpreter's muted microphone, to have the active interpreter send the word "Go" in the chat. This frees up the active interpreter to mute their microphone as needed: to cough, drink water, etc., without causing panic on the part of the non-active interpreter who doesn't know why the active interpreter is muting. Some interpreters also prefer, when they are the non-active interpreter, to un-mute their microphone before the actual moment of the handover; the only issue is that this runs the risk of both interpreters talking at once, which is the major problem you're trying to avoid.

- The main thing with remote handovers is to discuss them with your boothmate well ahead of the event start time, especially if you've never worked together before.

4.6: What I've Learned from Remote Court Interpreting

Since passing the Colorado French court interpreter certification exam, I've interpreted about 100 days a year in the Colorado state courts, and the courts of other states as well. I **love** the work, and I'm not saying that just in case one of my managing interpreters reads this. At first, my goal was simply to pass the court interpreter certification exam to prove to myself that I could do it (hello, imposter syndrome). But lo and behold, I find court work both fascinating and fulfilling; I love learning about the legal system and feeling like I'm serving as a bridge between French-speakers and the legal system. I just love everything about it.

Pre-pandemic, I honestly had some questions about the Colorado courts' emphasis on in-person interpreting. As in many states, Colorado court interpreters are paid for travel time (at half rate) and mileage, and our state is large. In many cases, we're driving an hour each way or more, sometimes for an appearance that might last five minutes. I sometimes wondered, is this really necessary? Might some of this be better handled remotely?

In some cases, remote court interpreting has worked really well, and it certainly expedites things. The court staff work really hard to keep things running smoothly, and in most cases, the remote systems work well enough that the hearings can happen. And it's true that for a simple scheduling hearing, it's much easier and more efficient to handle it remotely. However, I've also experienced various issues with remote court interpreting:

- Bad audio is a chronic problem; none of the states I interpret for have any technological requirements for people who appear in remote court. I've interpreted for people who were driving, walking in parks, sitting outside in public places, or in a house with a lot of background noise, making it incredibly hard to understand them.

- People talking over each other is another issue. Especially when you're on the phone with no video, there's really no way to get someone to stop talking, other than to try to tell them to stop, or to start talking over them.

- The remote process seems like it would expedite everything, but in some cases it doesn't. An example is when people call in to a Webex conference on the telephone rather than from a computer, so their phone number appears instead of their name on the meeting ID. This then requires someone (usually a court clerk or the judge) to go through each phone number, read the number out loud, and ask the person to un-mute themselves and say who they are, i.e. "Calling from 333-333-3333, this is Jack Smith and I'm the father of the victim in the Jones case."

- Confidentiality: I've interpreted for a few family court hearings that clearly would have been confidential if they were happening in person. In one case, one of the parties' children were clearly visible in the background of the video call while custody issues were being discussed, including details that the children really should not have been hearing. Children are prohibited from courtrooms, but none of the courts I interpret for require a party to a case to get childcare in order to take a video call.

- Appearances: Lots of people don't show up to remote hearings; anecdotally, the no-show rate seems much higher to me than the no-show rate for in-person hearings. Which raises the question: If you don't show up to a remote hearing because your phone battery died or you can't figure out how to use Webex, should that constitute failure to appear? Neither option seems like a good one. If it does constitute failure to appear, is it really fair for someone to face an additional charge because their phone battery died? If it doesn't constitute failure to appear, what prevents people from simply not showing up and claiming that they couldn't log on to the remote system?

- Public participation and oversight: The fact that most court cases are public is a really important component of the U.S. legal system. I spent hours sitting in court and taking notes when I was studying for the court interpreter exam, and you see all kinds of people (reporters, family members, law students, court reporting students, interpreting students) observing in court. Family court cases and some others are closed to the public, but in my experience it's quite common to see people watching court proceedings just for their own interest or education. In a remote system, it's not always clear how or if the public can participate.

- The simple fact of people not being in the same room causes some hassles: On several occasions I've needed to sight-translate things like plea agreements. Those have to be sent by e-mail, sometimes through multiple people, instead of being passed across a table. Then the defendants often have to sign the agreements via Docusign, which can be complicated since they're often using a phone rather than a computer. In order to maintain the proper flow of information (defendant-interpreter-district attorney-interpreter-defendant), the interpreter has to interpret all of those technical questions ("I don't see where I have to sign,"

"There's no yellow box," "The submit button isn't working") rather than someone helping the person right there.

In many situations, I think remote court interpreting falls into the "better than no interpreting" category. If everyone is patient and the technical side works out, things can go pretty well. Using a purpose-built RSI (remote simultaneous interpreting) platform, which at least some court systems are looking into, would make things even better. Still, I'm now more convinced of the merits of bringing an interpreter from an hour away to interpret for even short appearances!

4.7: On-Site Interpreting

The technical and sound aspects of on-site interpreting may seem like a no-brainer, but they can sometimes be even more complicated than remote interpreting because your speakers aren't sitting in front of a computer. Additionally, very few conference venues in the United States have interpreting booths (this is not the case in Europe, where fixed booths are a common feature of conference venues), and clients are often resistant to renting booths, instead putting interpreters at tables in the back of the room (for those of you who are accustomed to comfortable, sound-proof booths with a good view of the speaker, I'm not kidding here!).

In the U.S. market, it is also common for interpreters to use "tour guide" equipment, often referred to in Europe as "bidule," where the interpreters wear a headset and microphone attached to a transmitter and the participants wear headsets attached to a receiver, sometimes selecting between various channels for different languages. This system avoids having the interpreter interpret consecutively in front of the entire group, particularly if only some of the participants need to listen to the interpreting; and (for better or worse) the interpreter can interpret for speakers who aren't using microphones, which isn't the case if the interpreter is in a soundproof booth. I use this type of setup for a client that sends me to week-long on-site assignments to interpret in-person training courses where only a handful of the participants are French speakers. It's definitely more tiring than being in a booth and listening to speakers who are using microphones, but it suits the purpose of the training sessions very well. Tour guide equipment also allows the interpreter to move around the room to listen to different speakers, which can be useful in meetings where there is informal discussion among the participants.

One type of on-site interpreting that you should try to avoid is whisper interpreting, often referred to by its French name, *chuchotage*. Clients may ask you to do whisper interpreting when there are only a few participants who need to hear you, and/or when the client has forgotten about or ignored the fact that there will be an interpreter and thus there is no equipment available. The client may ask or suggest, "Maybe you could just sit behind the German (etc.) speakers and talk softly so that only they can hear you?" This sounds like a decent idea, and it can be the best or only option in situations where it would be inappropriate or impossible to use interpreting equipment. If you're interpreting during a business dinner, it would be bizarre/impossible to have the participants speak into microphones while you sit in a booth, so there are situations where whisper interpreting is the norm. But in standard meetings or conferences, whisper interpreting is problematic and to be avoided for a few reasons:

- Speech therapists will tell you that unless you've been specifically trained in proper whispering technique, whispering can be as stressful on your voice as shouting.

Speaking at any "unnatural" volume, whether very softly or very loudly, is really hard on your voice, particularly over long periods of time.

- It's almost impossible to whisper so that your intended listeners can hear you but everyone else cannot. In many chuchotage situations, you end up talking loudly enough that you're bothering other people around you who don't need the interpreting, or talking softly enough that your intended listeners have a hard time understanding you.

- Unless you're interpreting for only one or two people, it's also almost impossible to sit comfortably while whisper interpreting for a group.

Try to avoid whisper interpreting situations; sometimes (specifically, during meals) there is no good alternative, but the stress on your voice and the annoyance to participants is something you want to avoid.

4.8: The Traveling Interpreter

Big thanks to my friend and colleague Amélie Roy for suggesting this section! Working on written translations while traveling is pretty simple: you really just need a good enough internet connection to do online research and submit your translations. When I was exclusively a translator, I would even take work along on trips where there was little to no internet available, use my installed electronic dictionaries for research, then find a coffee shop or library with Wi-Fi to do any final research and submit the translation. Working as an interpreter while traveling is possible, but it involves a lot more advance planning and some additional equipment, so you want to strategize about this before you hit the road.

A major issue with remote interpreting is internet speed and stability. The tough part is that you can often get a sense of internet speed before you travel somewhere. For example, if you're renting an Airbnb or holiday apartment, you can often get the host to send you a screenshot of the lodging's internet speed test, which is easy to run online. The issue is that this doesn't tell you anything about internet stability; it only gives you a snapshot of the speed at one point in time. I've searched for an internet stability test tool online but have yet to find something that would give the types of statistics an interpreter would need.

Another factor is that, if at all possible, you really, really want to connect your interpreting computer to wired internet/ethernet, not Wi-Fi, for stability and bandwidth purposes. In some places (most notably, the vast majority of hotel rooms), it's actually impossible to do this, because there is no modem with ethernet ports in your room, and the room itself does not have wall-mounted ethernet ports.

The risk here is that you don't want to disappoint a client with bad sound or spotty connectivity. There's nothing worse than having an assignment go poorly because you can't hear well, the attendees can't hear you well, you don't have enough bandwidth to connect a second device to communicate with your boothmate, or any other number of problems that can result from subpar internet.

There are a few ways to address this:

- Try to avoid doing important assignments in uncertain setups. I simply do not do conference assignments from hotel rooms, for example. I might do a court assignment that I know is going to be short, where I'm the only interpreter, and where I know that (as is typical in the state courts where I interpret) it is not uncommon for participants in the cases to call in on the phone with no video. I've never had to do this, but for a hearing that is only going to last 5-15 minutes, that is going to be done in consecutive mode anyway and is simply administrative (usually continuing the case to a new hearing date), it wouldn't be the end of the world. That's not a setup that would work for a conference assignment, so I simply don't do those types of assignments over hotel Wi-Fi.

- Ahead of a trip, if you're renting lodging, explain to the host what you need in terms of internet and ask them to tell you honestly whether their setup is likely to fit your requirements. These days, many Airbnb hosts have had a lot of remote workers as guests and will be able to tell you whether their internet can support multiple video calls at once, for example.

- If available, consider working from a co-working office if you have to do an important assignment while you're traveling. Some co-working offices will rent you a conference room or small office by the day, and since this is what they do as a business, they should have a good idea of whether there are ethernet ports, soundproofing, etc.

- If you really have to work from a hotel, consider renting a conference room. This may cost extra, even a lot extra, but if your other choice is letting a client down, it's better to spend the money and get better internet and a setup where you can actually work well.

Before taking interpreting assignments while traveling, you also need to think about your own hardware. If you're going to be traveling for any length of time, you want to bring a backup headset (because your headset is a single point of failure; you can't interpret without it) and possibly a portable second monitor. Ahead of a month-long remote work trip, I purchased a Dell 14 portable monitor, and I love it. It cost about U.S. $300, it's about the thickness of my regular laptop screen (the portable monitor fits in my laptop case along with my laptop), and it runs power and data through one USB-C cable, so it doesn't require an additional electrical outlet, and you can use it while running your laptop off the battery. A second monitor allows you to avoid crowding all of your windows (the interpreting platform, your reference documents, glossary, etc.) onto a small laptop screen, and can be a huge help if you're working on the road.

CHAPTER 5

Marketing Your Interpreting Services

5.1: The Basics of How to Find Clients

Finding interpreting clients isn't incredibly complicated, it's just a lot of work. Instead of spending time researching creative marketing techniques, you want to focus on a mix of straightforward outbound marketing (applying to agencies, contacting direct clients) and inbound marketing (creating a basic online presence, networking with other interpreters).

When I started out as a translator in 2002/2003, I applied to over 400 translation agencies and it still took around 18 months until I had full-time work. Launching as an interpreter was a two-phase process for me: After I passed the Colorado state court interpreter exam in 2019, I immediately had a "captive audience" client because the Colorado state courts give preference to certified interpreters, there is a pretty high demand for French in the Colorado state courts, and there are only a handful of certified French interpreters in the state. This is something to consider: whether you can start out as an interpreter by obtaining a certification or credential that gives you access to an immediate client base with minimal marketing. Court interpreting is an obvious fit here (and having a court certification also opens the door to non-court legal interpreting such as depositions, attorney-client conferences, etc.), but there are other options: perhaps there is a hospital near you that still allows family members to act as interpreters (a practice that is now prohibited in most legal settings) and could use a professional interpreter; perhaps your local school district hasn't considered how to serve parents who don't speak English. "Captive audience" clients like this can be a good place to start so you can focus on offering high-quality interpreting services instead of on marketing.

Before marketing your interpreting services, you want to make sure you have the skills to do the job and that you have the technical setup if you're considering offering remote interpreting services. There are so many training programs out there for interpreting (many more than for translation, in my opinion) that I would encourage you to pursue *some type* of formal training before starting to work as an interpreter. The risk of not knowing what you're doing is simply too high.

Once you're ready to start marketing, you'll need to narrow down: what type of interpreting are you interested in and qualified to do, what types of clients need that service, and are you interested in remote, in-person, or both? Although you want to do some market experimentation and "see what sticks," you also need to approach clients with a specific pitch: I'm looking for medical interpreting work in my local area, I'm looking for remote conference interpreting work, etc.

5.2: Marketing to Interpreting Agencies

Many interpreters start out working primarily or exclusively for interpreting agencies. Some agencies handle both translation and interpreting, while others handle interpreting only. You can find interpreting agencies in a variety of ways:

- Through professional association directories. Never contact an agency using the contact information in a directory; it may be out of date, and the directory terms of service may prohibit using it for marketing purposes. Use the directory to get agency names only, then go to the agency's website to find out how to apply.

- Through an internet search. Look for "Interpreting agencies in Chicago," or "Medical interpreting agencies," etc.

- On LinkedIn. Do a search similar to an internet search or search for a job title that seems promising: "interpreter recruiter," "managing interpreter," etc.

- Through referrals from other interpreters. You don't want to poach other people's clients, but networking with other interpreters is a good way to find clients. Perhaps they work in a different language pair than you. Perhaps their clients are looking for more interpreters. Perhaps they need a boothmate.

Once you've found interpreting agencies to apply to, it's time to take action. If you're applying "cold" (not being referred by someone else or following up on a contact you made in person), go to the agency's website and look for a link like "Freelancers," "Work with us," "Join the team," etc., and follow the instructions there. Some agencies have an online portal that you use to apply, others have an e-mail address to submit your resume/CV; however you apply, don't expect to get work from them after the first contact. Create a follow-up system, such as:

- First contact: apply, using the instructions on the agency's website.

- One week later, if you haven't heard from them: use the general e-mail address on their website to follow up. Use a subject line such as, "Spanish interpreter: applied via your website," and say something like, "Hello, I hope that you at [name of agency] are doing well. I am an English/Spanish medical interpreter, and I applied via your website last week. I'm just following up to see if you need anything else from me, or what the next steps in the application process are? Thank you and I hope to hear from you soon!"

- One week after that, if you haven't heard from them: look for the agency's employees on LinkedIn. Send a connection request, to which you can add a 200-character note, and you can send five of these per month with the free LinkedIn account. Say something like, "Hello [name], I'm an English/Spanish medical interpreter and I recently applied via your website. I'd love to connect!" Then, if the person accepts your connection request (you will be able to see this in your LinkedIn connections), send a longer message, like the e-mail template above.

- To this, you could also add some creative follow-up if it's an agency you particularly want to work with. Send them a handwritten card in the mail ("I applied via your website and look forward to hopefully working together in the near future!") or ask for an informational interview ("To learn more about their business and how you might fit in") if they're in your local area.

When you do these follow-up steps, it's easy to feel like you're being a pest. Remember: Agencies need interpreters; they can't do business without you. Agencies aren't concerned about sparing your feelings. If they don't need your language, or if they only do legal interpreting, or if they only use people with a certification that you don't have, they'll tell you. And agencies cannot work with you if they don't know you. You have to go find them!

5.3: Marketing to "Captive Audience" Clients Such as Court Systems and Hospitals

If you are certified for court or healthcare interpreting, you may have access to some clients that are required or strongly encouraged to use your services. This can be a real plus when you are starting out as an interpreter because it gives you a built-in client base without having to market from scratch. Still, you want to cultivate these entities as potential regular clients rather than passively waiting for them to contact you.

Here's an example: after I passed the Colorado state court interpreter exam, a staff member in the Office of Language Access (an office that exists in many state court systems) sent a "Congratulations to our newly certified interpreters, here's their contact information!" e-mail out to all of the managing interpreters in the Colorado Judicial districts. I took this and ran with it; I followed up with my own, individual e-mail to each of the managing interpreters, inserting their names and copying a template message: "Hello Ana, I'm glad to be in touch with you! I'm a newly certified French interpreter based in Boulder. I'm available for remote and in-person assignments and I look forward to hopefully working with you soon." This resulted in a number of work offers, both in my local area and in other parts of the state.

If you have this type of "captive audience" client, I think the key is not to be complacent about being assigned work from them. Often, court systems and hospitals send out interpreter requests in a surprisingly low-tech way: a managing interpreter, interpreter coordinator, scheduler, bilingual services assistant, or someone else, simply sends an e-mail or makes a phone call, asking whether you are available for a given assignment. One of the ways to turn court or healthcare interpreting into a money-making endeavor is to do a lot of it, or to be one of the people who gets offers for longer and more lucrative assignments. In order to do this, you need to be one of the people who comes to mind when the scheduling person decides who to e-mail or call. In this way, courts and hospitals are not unlike any other type of client: you need to cultivate them in order to become one of their go-to interpreters.

5.4: Marketing to Direct Clients

Direct clients can take many forms. Lots of freelancers tend to think, "Fortune 500 company: way out of my league!" In reality, there are direct clients of all flavors and sizes. I interpret mostly through agencies and court systems, but I have a pretty eclectic variety of direct clients as well, including:

- A consulting company that does international business expert interviews. I do over-the-phone consecutive interpreting when they have a French-speaking expert and an English-speaking interviewer.

- A podcast about a historical event that happened in France. I interpret between French speakers who experienced or witnessed the event and the podcast host.

- A local NGO that collaborates with partners in West Africa who speak French. I do remote simultaneous interpreting for their quarterly conferences.

- Various law firms. There are only a few court-certified French interpreters in Colorado, so I do some deposition

and attorney-client conference interpreting for local
law firms.

Marketing to direct clients is more nuanced than marketing to
agencies. You have to figure out who might need you, who to contact, and how to contact them. This could be an entire book in and
of itself, but here's a crash course!

5.5: "Stealth" Marketing Opportunities

In addition to active marketing (applying to agencies and contacting direct clients) and passive marketing, there are lots of
ways to put out your marketing tentacles. One way to ensure a
steady flow of work in your interpreting business is to always be
marketing. That doesn't necessarily mean that you are actively
looking for work at all times, not least of all because you can't be
in two places at one time if multiple clients need you at once. But
you also don't want the feast-or-famine cycle that can result from
only thinking about marketing when you really need work. Here
are some ideas for "stealth" marketing ideas that you might want
to try:

Nudge Dormant Clients

- I like to call this "the world's most boring and the world's
  most effective marketing technique." Every couple of
  months, go through your old invoices and look for clients
  who you enjoyed working with but haven't heard from in
  a while. Send them a quick e-mail. "Hello, I hope you're
  doing well! In looking over my accounting records, I see
  that we haven't worked together since [include some details
  of the last assignment you did for them: "The public health
  NGO conference that I interpreted for in November," "The

orthopedics appointment I interpreted for in April"]. I'd love to work with you again, and I'm wondering whether you have anything in the pipeline that I might be helpful with. I look forward to hopefully working together again soon!" This sounds kind of ridiculous if you've never tried it. When I encourage freelancers to nudge their dormant clients, their typical reaction is often along the lines of, "That sounds annoying and it's going to irritate people! If they want to work with me, they know where to find me!" My plea is always to just try it on a few clients and let me know what happens. More often than not, the freelancer comes back with some surprising (to them!) results: "Welllll, what do you know! An interpreting agency I hadn't heard from in six months booked me for three days of work next month." "I had convinced myself that the managing interpreter hated me or that I had done something wrong in an assignment. But they immediately came back and offered a $1,500 assignment that was right up my alley." If you've never nudged dormant clients, start now!!

Use Availability Notifications to Remind Clients That You Exist

- This is like nudging, but centered around a specific time period. You could do this when you have an upcoming period with no assignments, when you're going on vacation or returning from vacation, or ahead of a major event like the Christmas/New Year's period in the Northern Hemisphere. You essentially do the same thing as described in the "nudging" section above, but mention a specific period of time: "I just wanted to check in and let you know that I'm fully available during the week of March 20 if you're looking to fill any German medical assignments."

"I'll be on vacation from June 1-15, but I look forward to working with you after that on any Italian conference assignments that may come up." "Ahead of the winter holidays, I wanted to update you on my availability for Spanish court assignments." This can be particularly useful if you are going to be working at a time of year (the month of August, mid-December to early January) that a lot of interpreters tend to take off.

Let Clients Know if You Earn a New Degree, Certificate, or Certification

- This is something that clients need to know! Any time you earn a new credential, e-mail all of your current and (perhaps even more importantly) potential clients to inform them. "I'm excited to let you know that I completed my Master's in conference interpreting." "I recently found out that I passed the New York state court interpreter certification exam." "I've earned my Core CHI credential."

Let Clients Know When You're Going to Be Attending a Language Industry Conference

- If you're going to be attending a conference sponsored by any professional association that includes interpreters, whether on a local, national, or international level, contact your current and potential clients to see if they will also be there and might like to meet up in person. Keep this low commitment: don't suggest a meal or anything else time-consuming unless this is one of your best clients and you're planning on treating them. Instead, say something like, "I'd love to just shake hands and put a name with a face; perhaps we could meet up during one of the coffee breaks?"

Post Interesting Things on LinkedIn

- LinkedIn is pretty much the go-to platform for professional networking, and in addition to developing a network of connections there, it can be really useful to post about things going on in your professional life. Any time you attend an interesting professional development event, write a short summary of it and post that on LinkedIn. This is also a great way to highlight any speakers whose presentations you particularly enjoyed. If you earn a new credential, post about that too!

5.6: How to Become a Go-To Interpreter

The goal of all of the above is to become a go-to interpreter: the person who clients think of and call on for regular and repeat assignments. It's a whole lot easier to manage 40 assignments a year from one good client than one assignment a year from 40 clients. Becoming a go-to interpreter first requires excellent interpreting skills. You can be a nice person but a sub-standard interpreter, and your niceness isn't going to balance out your lack of skills. Assuming you've worked on your interpreting skills enough that they are up to the job, here are some suggestions for becoming a client's favorite interpreter:

Always Be Early

- Not just on time--early. For online assignments, log on a few minutes *before* the connection time the client gave you so that you're in the waiting room when the organizer logs on. For in-person assignments, anticipate time-consuming issues: traffic, parking, getting through security, finding the room where you're working, getting the equipment set up. Allow more time than you think these things are going to take.

Always Be as Prepared as You Can Be

- If you don't have the meeting agenda, the speakers' presentations, etc., the time to ask for those is well ahead of the meeting, not when you log on or show up.

Always Arrange Turns and Handovers with Your Partner Before the Assignment

- In the sectors for which I interpret, 30-minute turns are typical. For online assignments, interpreters typically use a back-channel to do the handover (switching from one interpreter to another). See this book's section on remote interpreting for more on this. Make sure you have all of this worked out with your interpreting partner ahead of the assignment.

Always Remain Professional and Try to Be Easy to Work With

- It's fine to put a client on your "never again" list once the assignment is over, but no matter how poorly the assignment may be going, always remain professional and polite while you're working. The "easy to work with" part is nuanced, because you also want to avoid agreeing to do things you shouldn't do (interpret from bad audio, for example). But, within reason, you want to make life easy for the client, who has a lot of things in addition to the interpreting to take care of.

Express Appreciation to the Client, Particularly for Work You Enjoy

- When I invoice a client, I always add a "Thank you for your business" note. Additionally, after a particularly interesting assignment, I will often e-mail the client and tell them, "I really enjoyed X assignment, and I would love to interpret for that type of thing again in the future if the occasion arises."

Be a Good Boothmate

- When you work with a partner, it's easy to get competitive and insecure; that's just human nature. Often, the person is listening to every word you interpret, and no one is as critical as another interpreter. And yet, you're there to work together as partners and to make life easier, not harder, for each other. In addition to setting up turns and handovers, it can be useful to ask your partner whether they want you to help them out with terminology while they are interpreting, and if so, how. Particularly if I'm working with a French A interpreter (the opposite A language from me), I will pre-emptively tell them, "If you have any feedback or corrections for me after the assignment, it's much appreciated! One thing I love about our job is that there's always something to work on!"

5.7: Writing an Interpreter Resume/CV

A resume/CV is less critical these days than it used to be, but I would still recommend having an updated copy on hand, particularly if you want to apply to agencies. I'm not a resume-writing expert, and there are lots of good templates out there (try Canva.

com for nice one-page templates for infographic-style resumes), but here are some tips from experience:

Personally, I like to include my headshot photo on my resume. Make sure your headshot is professional (no selfies, no pets unless you interpret about animal-related topics or you're a veterinarian). It's also fine to not include a photo if you don't want to. I put my headshot photo in the upper left-hand corner of the resume.

Next, you need a headline, which should consist of, at a minimum, your name, your language pair(s), and what type of interpreting you do. I have my name on the first line, then below that, "French/English conference and legal interpreter."

The rest of your heading should include some sort of location information and contact information. For your location, it's not necessary to include your full address. Clients will ask for that if they need it. Rather, you want to put something that gives clients an idea of your time zone and geographic availability. I just put my city and state, or you could put "Boston metro area," or "Orange County, CA." For contact information, you need at least an e-mail address and a phone number. You want your e-mail address to look professional. It's best to buy your own domain name, even if you plan on using it only for e-mail. This is easy to do through any major domain registration service (I use GoDaddy.com, but there are lots of good domain registrars out there). If you're stuck on what domain name to buy, see if your name is available, or something like your name plus your language (corinnemckayfrench. com), or your name plus the word "interpreter." If you have a website, include it in your contact information section. More on websites later, but you could also substitute a good LinkedIn page for a website!

Next, you need a Profile or Summary section, because (sad but true!) many people aren't going to read the full text of even a one-page resume; they're just going to skim to get a sense of whether you're a fit for what they want. I would recommend three to six sentences, hitting the highlights of your skills and experience. Start with your languages (it's amazing how many people omit this basic information) and the type of interpreting you do: "Japanese/ English conference interpreter." "German/English medical and court interpreter." Then move on to any applicable certifications: "Certified by the Washington state courts." "CoreCHI healthcare interpreter certification." If you have an interpreting degree or certificate, definitely include that. If you have relevant experience, include a summary: "Court/legal interpreting experience includes arraignments, plea hearings, attorney-client conferences, motions hearings, trials, and depositions." "Medical interpreting experience includes medical, occupational therapy, and physical therapy appointments." I also think it's good, in the current business environment, to indicate whether you interpret online, in person, or both, and whether you're available for travel: "Full remote interpreting setup including soundproof room, wired internet, noise-cancelling microphone. Also available for on-site work and travel assignments."

Next, include either an Education and Credentials section or an Interpreting Experience section. What order to put these in depends on the significance of those two sections. If you just completed a Master's in conference interpreting but you have little to no interpreting experience outside your program, maybe you want to put the Education and Credentials section first to highlight that. If you are still working on your court certification but you have a lot of community interpreting experience, maybe you want to put the Experience section first.

It's always hard to know what to include in the Experience section when you don't have much experience. A couple of thoughts on that: you really shouldn't be looking for paid interpreting work if you have absolutely no experience. At the very least, you should do some sort of interpreter training and some assignments that are part of that program, or volunteer assignments. This is how I started out with conference interpreting: I did an interpreting program where we were required to interpret for the university's events as part of our classes, and then I got a referral to a non-profit environmental organization that was looking for pro bono interpreters, so by then I had five or six different conference events to list on my resume.

If you don't yet have a ton of experience, you may want to retitle the Experience section, something like "Recent medical interpreting assignments." This allows you to make an entire section out of a few assignments, because you can describe them in more detail: "Doctor-patient interpreting for a medical appointment involving a consultation for a total knee replacement."

How much other information to include depends on how much space you have left. Specifically, you'll need to decide whether to include past jobs that don't involve interpreting, if you have any. As a freelancer, gaps in your resume are not a major concern. Freelance clients are unlikely to ask about gaps, but it's up to you whether you want to include your full employment history or not. You may also want to include something about your extra-professional interests and any volunteer or charitable work. Other tips:

- Don't include anything religious or political (i.e. volunteer work for a political party or religious organization) unless you're OK with clients not working with you if their views differ from yours.

- One page is always best; two pages are the absolute maximum. Make sure to put the most important information on the first page.

- Testimonials from past clients or colleagues make a nice touch if you're looking to use up some space.

- I like to include the date on which I last updated the resume so that it looks current. I do this by putting one line at the very bottom of the second page, "Updated January 2025."

- Always send your resume as a PDF, never as a Word document. Give your file a descriptive name. I use "Corinne_McKay_French_2025," updating the file for the current year.

5.8: Creating a Basic Website

Websites are a big roadblock for a lot of freelancers, but a website is really helpful to your freelance business, even if you use it only passively, as something that just sits there that clients can look at if they want to know more about you.

One thing that's intimidating about making a website is budget. You can literally spend zero dollars or $10,000 (or more, or anything in between those two numbers) on a freelance website, depending on who you hire and what you want the website to do. Budget is a decent place to start: if you have a modest budget (which I would define as under about $1,500 and definitely under $1,000) and your computer skills are decent, I think you're better off creating a website using a website builder platform like Squarespace, WordPress, Wix, or Weebly, and putting your budget into some custom graphics that will make your website look unique. If your budget is more in the $2,000-$4,000 range, you can probably hire a good designer and get some custom graphics.

You also need to be clear on the purpose of your website: Is it meant to just sit there for clients to look at if they want to, or do you want it to pull clients to you, particularly for certain search terms? If so, you need to work with a designer who understands search engine optimization (SEO) or learn how to do at least basic SEO yourself. SEO is not dead, but you don't want to try to compete for broad terms like "Spanish interpreter." Instead, you want to pick targeted terms like "German interpreter Miami," or "Italian medical interpreter."

I think that a basic, professional website is fine for most free-lancers' purposes. It's also not the worst thing in the world to use a good LinkedIn profile as a de facto website, but just remember that, just like every other online platform, LinkedIn's business model involves listing the profiles of interpreters with similar qualifications right next to yours.

Your basic, professional website can consist of just a few pages:

Home

- Clearly state your name, languages, credentials, and location. In case clients already know that they want to contact you, make sure that you either list your contact information on the Home page or have a prominent link to the contact page. A photo of you interpreting makes a nice touch! Don't crowd the Home page with too much text, and don't overload it with long paragraphs of information about yourself. That's for the About page. Instead, stick to the information that you would put in the summary or Profile section of your resume/CV.

About

- Here's where you get to talk about yourself in more detail. However, you want to aim this section at the client's needs. I tell freelancers over and over again, no one cares about your life story. Once you get to know the client you can tell them how you won the seventh grade French award, or how you learned Russian on your grandmother's knee. In your website About section, try to address why the client should hire you, what sets you apart, what credentials you hold and what they mean, what types of interpreting work you do, what locations you serve, and whether you do remote interpreting.

Services

- Here's where you talk in more detail about the types of interpreting work that you do. Don't assume that clients understand our industry lingo: state whether you do simultaneous, consecutive, or both, what settings you interpret in, your remote interpreting setup, etc.

Contact

- Don't make clients hunt for how to contact you. I'm also not a huge fan of contact forms without direct contact information. If the client has an assignment for tomorrow, they don't want to fill out a contact form and wait for you to get back to them; they want to e-mail or call you right then. I think a contact form is fine in addition to your direct contact information, but not instead of your direct contact information.

Other Information

- I think it's nice to put a headshot photo on your website. For interpreting work, the client is likely to find out what you look like anyway, and I think it makes your site look more personal. Testimonials from past clients make a nice impression too!

Domain names cause many freelancers a lot of stress. I think that if your name (corinnemckay.com) is available, that's the easiest and least restrictive option. Next would be your name plus your non-native language (corinnemckayfrench.com) or your name plus the word "interpreter" (corinnemckayinterpreter.com). Just be careful with getting something that specifies a location or specialization (corinnemckaycolorado.com, corinnemckaymedicalinterpreter.com) because these may change throughout your career.

5.9: Creating a Basic LinkedIn Profile

In the U.S., LinkedIn is the primary professional networking platform and you should create at least a basic profile. Even if you use it only passively, for clients to see who you are and learn a little more about you, being on LinkedIn is something that showcases you as a serious professional interpreter.

You can work on your LinkedIn profile over time, but you could start with:

A Good Headshot

- This could be done by a professional photographer or by a friend with a good camera. Make sure you are dressed in professional clothes and that there is nothing distracting in the background.

A Descriptive Headline

- This sounds basic, but make sure to put your language pair(s), spelled out. Many people just put "Freelance interpreter," (which tells the client almost nothing about whether you are who they need) or use abbreviations that only other language people will understand ("Court interpreter SP<>EN"). Instead, use something like "Medical interpreter: English-Spanish and Spanish-English."

A Solid About Section

- You want to use keywords that are specific to what you do (court-certified Spanish interpreter, German conference interpreter) while avoiding a laundry list of your accomplishments and certifications. Remember that very few clients understand what interpreters and translators really do, and *do* not bog the client down in industry jargon. Something like, "I am a federally certified Spanish court interpreter, providing spoken language interpreting services to courts and law firms," is good; it's explanatory but not eye-glazing. Personally, I like putting "spoken language interpreting services," or even signifying that with a microphone emoji, because most clients don't know the difference between translation and interpreting. I also think that some sort of call to action is helpful: "Connect with me if you'd like to discuss your upcoming French interpreting needs." Numbers can be really powerful: "Last year, I provided over 200 days of interpreting services, about half of them in the New York state courts, and half for private-sector clients." Just keep it concise, positive, and focused on how your skills help clients, not the story of how you learned Russian on your grandmother's knee.

Some Recommendations

- Recommendations are powerful because, on LinkedIn, you can see them associated with a real person's profile; they can't be anonymous. This is also why it can be a challenge to obtain LinkedIn recommendations, but you can start by at least *writing* recommendations for interpreting colleagues, who may in turn do the same for you.

CHAPTER 6

How Might Interpreting Be Affected by AI?

6.1: Machine Interpreting and Other Technologies

As of this writing, ChatGPT has been on the scene for about two and a half years and various AI-related technologies are appearing on the scene. Some interpreters greet these changes with enthusiasm (being able to quickly gather information about obscure topics or machine-translate the text of a speech); some interpreters remain resistant to them and even fearful of these changes.

Accurate, pleasant machine interpreting of unscripted, live events (including court and medical encounters) is still not a reality. Personally, I believe that the "magic headset" (put on these special earphones and listen to the judge/doctor/conference speaker in another language) is probably beyond the working lifetime of those of us active in the language professions today. But there's still a lot going on. I'm a member of the online community techforword (techforword.com), and I find it really helpful for keeping up with technology developments. Whether you love, hate, fear, or are indifferent to AI, I think the worst option is to refuse to learn about it.

Automated captioning of live speech and automated translation of live captions has gotten a lot better in recent years. I do think that we'll see clients moving toward this type of arrangement (captioning videos into other languages) if they have videos with studio-quality audio, where the speakers are talking relatively slowly and clearly, there's no background noise, and a human can clean up the inevitable mistranslations plus work out idioms, jokes, etc. Tools such as Happy Scribe (happyscribe.com) are already doing this: automatically generating a video transcript in the original language, then automatically translating into a language that you select, while giving you the option to make changes before burning the captions onto the video.

In my opinion and experience, automated captioning works less well when (as is true in about 90% of the situations we interpret for) the speakers are not talking slowly or clearly, there's background noise, or the speakers are using humor, sarcasm, innuendo, etc. I recently did an interpreting job for a hybrid event, where some participants were attending in person and some others, including the interpreters, were remote. We were having trouble hearing people speaking into the tabletop microphones, so the organizers suggested that we turn on the automated captions in Zoom (not a bad suggestion on the face of it). However, this proved more distracting and confusing than helpful. In one instance, a participant was referring to the Americans with Disabilities Act, the ADA. The automated caption displayed, "the eighty A," which was not only unhelpful but caused even more confusion as we tried to figure out what this "eighty A" thing might be.

If you talk to clients about machine interpreting, I feel it's important to be realistic: AI tools can be really helpful for certain tasks (distilling huge volumes of information, generating ideas for big-picture strategic questions), but tend to fail when a task requires subtlety, creativity, decorum, humor…all the things that we do all day as interpreters.

At present, machine interpreting is, in general, way behind the quality of machine translation. But I would argue that the incentives to bypass human interpreters are greater. Interpreting is, in general, expensive and logistically complex: think about the amount of time that is devoted just to interpreter scheduling and how many people would like to eliminate that by just having a "magic earpiece" that a hospital patient or court defendant could put on, regardless of the risks to accuracy, confidentiality, empathy, or anything else. We'll have to see where this heads in future years!

6.2: Tools for Interpreting Prep

There are various computer-assisted tools for interpreting preparation out there, with the main feature being automated glossary creation. A good place to start is InterpretBank (interpretbank.com), which allows you to use AI in a few ways: to generate glossaries from documents you already have, from a specific web page, or on a topic of your choice (examples on their website include "solar energy," and "the Roman empire"). I haven't tried InterpretBank, but I've heard good things about it from other interpreters.

If you're interested in interpreting technology in general, I highly recommend Josh Goldsmith's online platform techforword (techforword.com). Having a techforword membership (and this is not an affiliate deal!) allows me to simply read their articles and attend their webinars versus doing my own research on technology tools for interpreting.

6.3: **Where Is All of This Headed?**

As stated above, I personally believe that we'll see more clients moving toward the use of AI and machine interpreting tools, regardless of whether this is a good idea. I think that, as word people, we often ask the wrong question, focusing on whether machine translation or machine interpreting are comparable to the quality of a human translator or interpreter (generally not), rather than on how we talk to clients about these differences in a way that makes sense to them, and how we find clients who perceive and are willing to pay for the quality that trained, professional human interpreters provide.

In closing, I believe that the future of interpreting belongs to people with diverse businesses who work for clients who care. If you do only one thing, for only one type of client, it's a good idea to branch out so that you're less subject to the "single point of failure" risk. We saw this at the beginning of the COVID pandemic: a not-insignificant number of interpreters ended up leaving the profession because none of their clients were quick to pivot to remote interpreting, they had no other source of income, and they were left in a stressful financial situation. Interpreters who had at least some remote clients, or who did at least some translation alongside interpreting, or had another aspect to their freelance businesses (language teaching, voiceover, editing, copywriting), fared much better.

If you work for clients who are only using you because they have to, it's also a good idea to branch out. If your clients are happy with "kind of/sort of good enough," they may see some flavor of machine interpreting as satisfactory for their needs, even if it leaves the people they serve (customers, patients, etc.) underserved and disrespected. Working for clients who see you as a critical part of the team will be key to thriving as these new technologies continue to unfold!

In Conclusion

If you've made it this far, I hope that you've gotten some useful information from this book. I often feel that succeeding as a translator or interpreter is half *mentality* (believing you can do it) and half *practicality* (learning how to do it). I hope that this book has given you some encouragement in both of those ways. I also feel that reading this book indicates that you *have the courage to try*. I often tell people that, because I feel strongly that it's true, many people never even know what they're capable of in life because they're too afraid to try. They get derailed by the "what ifs." What if it doesn't work out, what if I don't like it, what if I try and I'm not good enough? I firmly believe that if you try to achieve a big goal, something positive will come of it, even if it doesn't work out exactly the way that you hoped. I'm cheering you on in your efforts, and I'm proud of you for having the courage to try.

I see a bright future for the interpreting profession, definitely including new technological advances that will augment, but not replace, the skills of human interpreters. When I talk to bilingual people in their 20s who have an interest in translation or interpreting, I encourage them to go for it, although the professions have changed a lot since I started in 2002. Interpreting has many incredible aspects: two things I really love are that there's always something new to learn or work on, and you can craft an interpreting career that fits your financial and life goals, whether that's an in-house job or freelancing very part-time. Whatever your big crazy dreams are, I hope that this book has nudged you toward them! If you have comments or suggestions for the next edition of this book, e-mail me at corinne@translatewrite.com; all feedback is welcome!

Corinne McKay

Boulder, Colorado

February, 2025

Acknowledgments

A mid-life career pivot is no small undertaking, and I am incredibly grateful to everyone who supported and encouraged me in this big, crazy dream. Melinda Gonzalez-Hibner, Judy Jenner, and Cris Silva cheered me on when I was still in the "Am I crazy??" idea stage. Athena Matilsky patiently coached me through a year of preparation for the state-level court interpreting exam and was the first person who mentioned the Glendon College MCI program to me. Julia Poger, Chris Guichot de Fortis, and all of the instructors in the 2020 Cambridge Conference Interpreting Course provided a middle-aged, not-very-confident court interpreter with an incredible opportunity to explore conference interpreting. Xiang Gu told me that the Glendon program was going online and encouraged me to apply. Glendon program director Andrew Clifford organized a year of top-notch interpreting training in the middle of a pandemic, and our instructors Qjinti Barrios van der Valk, Helen Campbell, Ahmed El Khamloussy, Andy Gillies, Xiang Gu, and Michelle Hof did an incredible job of teaching us online in a whole new environment. I will always be grateful for the friendship and support of my Glendon cohort, especially Sandra Aidar-McDermott, Nairi Khandjian, and the world's best boothmate, Amélie Roy, who also provided the inspiration for the "Traveling interpreter" information in this book. Finally, none of this would be possible without my family; my parents LaNelle and Bruce, who instilled in me the courage to try, my daughter Ada, without whom life would be no fun at all, and my husband Dan, who has been putting up with and even encouraging my big, crazy dreams for 25+ years and isn't done yet!

About the Author

Corinne McKay has been a full-time freelancer since 2002; she is certified by the American Translators Association for French to English translation and by the Colorado Judicial Branch for French court interpreting. She holds an M.A. in French Literature from Boston College and a Master of Conference Interpreting from Glendon College. In addition to her own translation and interpreting work, Corinne runs the online professional development platform Training for Translators (trainingfortranslators.com).

www.ingramcontent.com/pod-product-compliance
Lightning Source LLC
Chambersburg PA
CBHW020201090426
42734CB00008B/898